# Advance Praise for
## *Wealth Mismanagement*

"I have known Ed for over forty years and he has always had an empathy chip that has served his clients well and allowed him to rise as one of the financial services industries stars. This book is the best at helping investors determine if what they have is what they need."

—Dennis Greenwald, Former General Counsel, Morgan Stanley

"Ed has written a very down to earth, easy-to-read book that will benefit everyone, regardless of net worth. I encourage all to read this and adopt the CHIP score in all your investment decisions."

—Peter Berg, Iconic Hollywood Director and Actor

"Ed Butowsky's *Wealth Mismanagement* provides investors with a practical and meaningful approach to creating an investment portfolio that will meet individual needs in retirement or otherwise. Often using autobiographical anecdotes, Ed provides an easy-to-understand, unvarnished review of why individual investment portfolios proffered by Wall Street institutions frequently fall shy of meeting an investor's long-term financial needs, and how to remedy that circumstance.

"If you are interested in preserving and enhancing your wealth over time, I recommend you buy and study this book."

—John Williams, Founder, ShadowStats

"Mixes entertaining personal stories with smart observations on the markets. Even Wall Street pros will learn new insights."

—Rich Karlgaard, Publisher, *Forbes*,and Author of *Late Bloomers:The Powerof Patience in a World Obsessed with Early Achievement*

"I have been a client of Ed's for nearly twenty years. He has always put my interest first and this book puts the investor's interest first. After reading this book, you will understand if you have what you need in your portfolio. A fantastic read and one that will keep all financial advisors on their heels."

—Joe Phillips, Serial Entrepreneur and Philanthropist

"Ed's not afraid to tell the truth. This book proves it. I have trusted and relied on Ed for years and he has always stood by his word. Pick up this book and see if your current portfolio has the characteristics you were needing."

—Kris "Tanto" Paronto, American Author and Speaker as well as a former US Army Ranger and CIA Security Contractor

"As an industry compliance professional for forty-seven years, I can vouch that this book was written through an investor's lens and should be used to hold your current advisor accountable for their recommendations. This CHIP score, which is introduced in this book, will be the industry standard one day. Hop on it early. Sadly, your current advisor will not be happy you read this book."

—Rhenée Rogé, CEO, Securities Broker Dealer and Investment Advisor Consulting

"I have never had bad financial advice from Ed—he is always spot on and ahead of the pack. This book is one not to miss."

—Lara Logan, Award-Winning Foreign Correspondent for CBS's *60 Minutes*

"Ed is a good friend and mentor who has taught me a lot about finances. It's always good when you can sleep well at night knowing your money is in good hands. This is a must-read book and it will help you navigate through the fears we all have about investments."

—Torii Hunter, MLB Legend and All-Star

"If you have ever wondered how to truly evaluate how good of a job your advisor is actually doing, Ed's book provides you with the tools necessary to find out. His candid insight reveals the lack of true risk mitigation being provided by many advisors in the industry today. It is a must read for anyone concerned with protecting their assets."

—Benjamin Fujihara, Former Morgan Stanley Managing Director, Former Complex Director, Complex Council Member

"I don't make financial move without running it by Ed Butowsky. This book will keep you from swinging at a bad 'pitch.'"

—Cliff Floyd, MLB All-Star and Current Sirius XM announcer

# WEALTH
## MISMANAGEMENT

# WEALTH
## MISMANAGEMENT

A Wall Street Insider on the
Dirty Secrets of Financial Advisers
and How to Protect Your Portfolio

# ED BUTOWSKY
### WITH DENNIS KNEALE

Post Hill
PRESS

A POST HILL PRESS BOOK

Wealth Mismanagement:
A Wall Street Insider on the Dirty Secrets of Financial Advisers
and How to Protect Your Portfolio
© 2019 by Ed Butowsky with Dennis Kneale
All Rights Reserved

ISBN: 978-1-64293-234-8
ISBN (eBook): 978-1-64293-235-5

Cover art by Cody Corcoran
Interior design and composition by Greg Johnson, Textbook Perfect

**Post Hill Press**
New York • Nashville
posthillpress.com

Published in the United States of America

*This book is for Dani,*
*for her love and unwavering support*
*through every step of my life and career.*

# Contents

# Foreword

For the better part of three decades I have been a wealth manager focused on protecting and growing the portfolios of my clients in an investing world ruled by the rival impulses of fear and greed. That term—wealth manager—also means I have been my clients' psychotherapist, rabbi, crisis counselor, and cheerleader, through times good and bad, scary and giddy.

I started my career with Morgan Stanley & Co. and spent almost twenty years at the fabled Wall Street investment bank, presiding over the personal fortunes of hundreds of rich clients, tech entrepreneurs, professional athletes, and other investors. Ultimately I shepherded the placement and protection of $11 billion in other people's money. And while that might evoke Hollywood visions of Gordon Gekko furiously trading a hundred times a day, my investments had all of a 5 percent turnover in a year.

In 2005, after a career on Wall Street, I opened my own firm in search of a better way to serve clients and build their wealth. Only now can I tell you the truth about something that has bugged me and embarrassed me for years.

Finally it is time to admit it: Wall Street wealth advisers and the "bulge bracket" giants who dominate the business are failing their clients. In most every way that counts, they are falling short. The financial advice business is dysfunctional, self-absorbed, occasionally venal, and almost always kind of clueless. The people who earn princely sums to manage the wealth of their even-richer clients are good people who mean well, for the most part. They want to do a good job, and they believe they are doing a good job. But they are delusional.

They do what their Wall Street firms have told them to do, and they have been taught the wrong things to do by people who don't know the right things to do. They haven't been trained in the most basic concepts of portfolio construction and how to measure and manage risk. They have little appreciation for some of the most important factors in managing money (risk, volatility, and cost-of-living increases), and they barely know the true financial needs of their clients.

The stock brokers and money managers and financial advisers who are supposed to be taking care of your money—taking care of your future and your family—have no idea what they are doing. I will say it again, in a gentler way: Most people in the money management business are unknowledgeable in how best to advise you. Even worse, they don't know that they don't know. Nor do their firms train them in even the most basic rules for how to manage a portfolio.

This image is exactly the opposite of what most American investors have in mind when they think of a Wall Street financial adviser, thanks to twenty or thirty years of brainwashing by soft-lens, stentorian TV commercials featuring caring brokers in pinstripes and wire-rim spectacles.

The implications of this ignorance are ominous and disturbing. Millions of Americans are committing financial suicide, passively, gradually, and unwittingly. Their advisers are leading them down a path to ruin, slowly and imperceptibly, failing to shield them from the hazards of market turmoil and volatile business conditions, and unable to capitalize on shifts in investor sentiment.

Thus, financial advisers across the nation are reassuring their clients and telling them don't worry, it's okay, you are in good shape when you *should* worry (about the right things), it *isn't* okay, and chances are your portfolio is in *bad* shape. All of this makes me seethe with anger and outrage—leavened with no small amount of chagrin for any part that I might have played in perpetuating it. Nobody should go to bed unaware of the risks of what might happen to their portfolios overnight or in the future. Yet people across the US are vulnerable.

Their "expert" advisers have no idea how to assess the maximum downside risk required to get the returns necessary for them to retire in comfort and preserve their savings. In the next crash—and there always will be a next crash—American retirees will be left "Naked and Afraid" (as the survivalist reality show would put it), unprotected because most people on Wall Street haven't been trained to know any better.

This has been going on for decades, and it hasn't changed. Until now. I wrote this book to save you from the bad brokers and money managers in the business, which is pretty much all of them. My aim is to shine a glaring light on the problems in the business and why they persist, and then offer you one simple, basic tool that will give you control over your investments and put your broker to shame. I want to empower you, the client, to protect yourself.

## Introducing the CHIP Score

That simple tool is called the CHIP Score, for Chapwood Investment Portfolio Score, derived from the name of my financial advisory firm. For twenty years I have been thinking about risk and volatility, and how to quantify them, mulling the real increase in the cost of living compared with the real returns a portfolio earns. This tool is my answer, and I have spent many years devising it, testing it, fine-tuning it and, ultimately, deploying it. You can do-it-yourself, and the CHIP Score can empower you to fix your portfolio and reconstruct it in a way that can make it a lot less vulnerable to the next market rout.

My CHIP regimen also can help you assess whether your adviser is failing in his or her basic mission: to keep your assets protected and safe, yet able to grow at maximum output while assuming only moderate risk. By answering just fourteen questions and data inputs, you can quantify the risk in your portfolio, gauge your returns compared with the rise in your cost of living, assess the extent of diversification and downside protection—and evaluate the true performance of your financial advisers.

Everything you are about to read is true, and it may make you feel as angry as it has made me feel. The difference is that after you finish reading this book, you can do something to fix this mess.

\* \* \*

In the old days we were known as registered reps, and later the preferred term was broker. As the once-rarified business exploded in the early 1980s into one gigantic sales machine, promoting the same kinds of financial products to all kinds of customers, Wall Street firms looked for fancier titles. The firms were forbidden from calling us portfolio managers because we had no portfolios to manage (and they hadn't bothered to instruct us in how to do so, regardless), so they chose the highfalutin moniker wealth managers. Even though we didn't know the first thing about managing wealth.

Rather than customize a portfolio expressly for one client's particular needs, Wall Street shills opted for one-size-fits-all templates aimed mainly at selling their firms' products rather than serving their customers. The "bulge-bracket" firms that employ them—including Morgan Stanley, Goldman Sachs, J. P. Morgan Chase, Merrill Lynch & Co. (now part of Bank of America), and a few other titans—spend hundreds of millions of dollars a year on world-class research. Yet most wealth managers spend little time reading it; they focus on landing new accounts and lining their own pockets.

When I joined Wall Street, I was a young man with untested skills. My first day as a full-time broker in the Dallas office of Morgan Stanley was momentous and portentous: Terrible Tuesday, as the *Wall Street Journal* later would dub it, the day after Black Monday, October 19, 1987, when the Dow Jones stock average plunged 22.6 percent in a single day, setting off a worldwide financial crisis. It remains, by far, the worst decline in the history of the two-hundred-year-old New York Stock Exchange. (In the crash that preceded the Great Depression of 1929, stocks fell 12.8 percent in a single day.)

That morning, pulling up to the firm's rather unremarkable fifteen-story building on Akard Street in downtown Dallas, my over-riding concern was where to find a parking space. Soon after I entered the office, something felt gravely wrong. "Oh shit-shit-shit!" one broker shouted.

"That's not normal," I thought to myself, as other brokers, looking shocked and shaken, fielded calls from frightened clients. It felt like I had walked into a war zone. Later I would realize: they could have avoided panicking when stocks plunged if they had adjusted properly for risk in their clients' portfolios by offsetting potential declines with other kinds of investments (bonds, gold, real estate, more exotic *alternatives*).

In the ensuing years, as stocks rebounded and embarked on a bull market of historic proportions (both in terms of how high stocks would rise and how long the run would continue), I learned the uncomfortable truth of how the industry works. I saw how basically every firm was the same. Merrill Lynch created (and patented) the CMA (cash management account), and everyone followed in pursuit. Merrill would come out with a new mutual fund idea, and every other brokerage firm would replicate it and sell it to all comers, no matter how divergent their needs.

The better I got at the job, the more disillusioned I became with the yawning gap between how well we *thought* we were serving clients and how poorly we were doing at protecting them and enriching them. I felt like I was on a bandwagon. I saw lots of people doing what I did. We sat in these big fancy offices at a big-name firm, and all of us were utterly convinced that we were doing a good job.

Not a single moment of our training regimen, if you could call it training, was spent on portfolio design, diversification, or risk reduction. Instead, we spent our time learning about the mutual funds (baskets of various stocks) that our employers were creating and the fees we were charging to sell them to our clients.

When clients hire an adviser, their number one priority is "Take care of me and make sure you don't lose my money," and the weird thing is, nobody at the titanic Wall Street houses ever taught us how to do that, not really. Yet clients to this day are unaware of this weakness. When they need heart surgery, they pick the best surgeon they can find and insist he or she have the best possible training and experience; yet, blindly, they put their money in the control of brokers who are untrained in how to protect them.

### 'Golden Retrievers'

All these firms wanted their brokers to gather money and give it to them to manage by selling their inventory of financial products. We were "golden retrievers," as a colleague once put it, unleashed to go out and gather the gold and bring it back to our masters.

We did this rapaciously and with an unintentional and unknowing lack of regard for preserving our clients' wealth, although a lot of us failed to realize this at the time (and most advisers on Wall Street remain oblivious to it). We were uninformed about the vagaries of real inflation and how it eats away at investors' savings, and we were ill-equipped to spot risk, measure it, assess it, and, especially, offset it.

Because nobody knew how to construct and manage a portfolio properly, we also were unable to devise an objective way to evaluate the effectiveness of its design. If we don't know which important things we don't know, how can we begin to know whether we have protected our clients adequately?

Nor were regulators any better at this stuff. The Securities and Exchange Commission (SEC) and the industry's self-regulatory body, FINRA (the Financial Industry Regulatory Authority), lack a specific prescription for evaluating risk and volatility, and for judging whether Wall Street firms are adequately safeguarding client accounts. The securities industry is heavily regulated, and it is heavily self-policed, but its obsessive focus on "compliance" exists for a sole reason: to cover the assets (and asses) of investment firms and insulate them from investor lawsuits. Protecting the client is, for most advisers, almost an afterthought.

And if the regulators don't understand it, why would the money managers under their watchful eyes be able to understand it, much less the clients? As this realization crept up on me in recent years, I felt like the entire system I had served for three decades was a fraud.

Clients see only one metric: whether their wealth is up, and by how much, compared with the holdings of everybody else. That is only the crudest measure, and it can be an insufficient and misleading one. Just as important are such factors as: How much risk did you take on to reap the returns you reaped? Was your portfolio diversified with non-correlated assets that run counter to the broader markets? Were you able to narrow the range of possible investment outcomes to reduce volatile swings in the value of various asset classes your account? What was your *real* rate of return after deducting management fees, administrative costs, and taxes? Did it keep up with the rise in your cost of living in the past year?

Until now, investors have been missing a good, clear way to evaluate how well their financial advisers are doing at constructing a strong and safe portfolio, evaluating risk and reducing it, and adding offbeat, alternative investments that zig when the rest of the market zags. My new CHIP Score empowers you to quantify, measure, and track those factors and more.

Nobody else is looking out for you. Reject from inception the idea that your typical financial adviser can safeguard your portfolio and protect you from loss; they are unable to protect you given that they are untrained and uninformed in how to do so. You must look out for yourself, and this book will teach you a new way, and a much better way, to do that.

# CHAPTER 1

# Wary from the Start

In some ways, my career on Wall Street began as a fit of youthful rebellion, sparked by a dare, a challenge thrown down by my father. He had made his career as a well-regarded lawyer and regulator for the SEC in Washington, and once I graduated from the University of Texas in Austin, he mentioned he could set up an interview for me at Morgan Stanley, should I ever so desire.

Some time later, I had no choice but to ask him about it. I was unemployed, having been fired from my first job out of college, and I was staying in a storage unit on the outskirts of Austin because the rent was incredibly cheap. So I drove to the Barton Creek Square mall, walked to the payphone beneath the main escalator, made the call to my dad, and asked him to arrange the Morgan interview; I was ready to become a stockbroker. His response still resonates three decades later: "Son, I'll get you an interview, but you're never gonna be any good at this."

That hurt me, it all but destroyed me, and I thought, "What a shitty thing to say to your son." Instead of saying that and getting into an unnecessary spat, I said, "Dad, just let me give it a shot," before admitting, "I don't know what else to do."

Like most fathers and sons, my dad and I had a complex relationship. He was a fierce man, blunt-spoken in the way real men used to be (without getting accused of the toxic masculinity that offends some sensitive souls these days). He had grown up in Philadelphia and never knew his own father, and he had worked hard all his life. While attending law school, he worked three different jobs at once, bagging groceries, working in a pharmacy, and landing a coveted slot on the law review at the George Washington Law School, in the same month in which his third child was born (that would be yours truly).

When my dad entered the room, he owned it. He could be demanding, and I could be ornery on occasion, determined to prove him wrong, especially regarding any doubts he held about me.

My father agreed to set up the introduction to Morgan Stanley on one condition: "If I get you an interview, it's going to be in New York, and if you succeed you're going to be in New York." That is where he was based. Only years later did I realize that my father, in telling me I would never be "any good at this," sought to provoke me into joining the firm to prove him wrong. Though he might never say so outright, he wanted his son to move back to New York to be closer to him and my mom (they had divorced a couple of years earlier).

I wish I had realized this at the time. Life is poorly organized. By the time you finally know the things you are supposed to know—such as the notion that my dad wanted me home and dared not admit it— you already have lived through those moments, and it is too late. You can try to apply those lessons to future events, but often new lessons are needed, unknown in the moment and to be learned only afterward, when yet again it is too late.

And, yes, this also is an apt description of the ups and downs of investing.

I would join Morgan Stanley, but only after ginning up a scheme that let me move from New York back to Texas, where I would spend the rest of my career (thus far, anyway). From the moment I started cold-calling local business owners in the Southwest to start building my book of new clients for Morgan Stanley, I was wary of the business.

This wariness runs deep in me, maybe down to my DNA. I was born in Silver Spring, Maryland—a bedroom community for people commuting to government jobs nearby in Washington D.C. My father, David Martin Butowsky, was the head of enforcement at the SEC from 1962 until 1970.

At the SEC, it was my father's mission to make sure what Wall Street did was right, that it followed the rules. Because of his job, I met my first financial swindler when I was all of thirteen years old—in fact, the man taught me to play craps. Weird, right?

His name was Robert Lee Vesco, and he was an infamous fugitive financier who had fled the US to Costa Rica in 1973, amid allegations that he had looted an investment company and stolen almost a quarter of a billion dollars of investors' money. (That is $1.6 billion in today's dollars). He also was wanted for making an illegal $200,000 campaign contribution to President Nixon's run for re-election in 1972 using, as his middleman, the president's nephew, Donald Nixon, whom Vesco had employed as a gofer to gain an "in" at the White House.

By the time Vesco went on the lam, my father had left the SEC and moved to New York to form his own firm. A federal judge appointed him to be a special counsel and investigate Vesco's many shady deals and who else had been profited—all of this while Robert Vesco and half a dozen of his henchmen were fugitives in Central America and beyond the reach of the law.

## Catch Him If You Can

Their cat-and-mouse courtship over the ensuing four years is worthy of a Hollywood script, a la *Catch Me If You Can*. As my dad pursued Vesco in Costa Rica, Colombia, the Bahamas, and Cuba, questioning him and seizing assets along the way, they would end up developing a begrudging admiration for each other and building a friendship that no one else knew existed.

Vesco enjoyed teasing my dad, in a good-natured way, sending him a birthday cake on his birthday for a few years running. Vesco called him "The Whale," a joking reference, apparently, to my dad's ample girth. Never did my father lose sight of the flawed character of the man he was pursuing. As he would note in 1977 in the opening of his final report on the case, spanning more than nine hundred pages:

"This report is lengthy, its subject complex, but let there be no mistake about it; the Report demonstrates that Robert Vesco is a thief."

You have heard of the Ponzi schemer Bernie Madoff, exposed in the financial collapse of 2008. He fleeced his investors for more than ten billion dollars, but all he did was *pretend* to trade. Robert Vesco was far more audacious and industrious. He did deals for real, and he had so many fingers in so many pies on all sides of the deals that he would have made a great investment banker at the Goldman Sachs of today. He was a hard bargainer, manipulative and shrewd, and aggressive as hell. As Dad put it:

"Vesco is obsessed with control over persons, transactions, and events. He has a keen perception of how to influence people. He has a superb intellect and is able to master virtually any given problem to suit his own ends no matter how complex and no matter what ethical considerations may be present. He has a magnetism which attracts people to him and he utilizes whatever additional leverage may be available to turn them into adherents to his cause."

A Detroit-born high school dropout, Vesco moved to New Jersey and later parlayed a bank loan into a controlling stake in a small, publicly held valve-maker named International Controls Corp. In 1970 he used ICC to take control of a troubled investment company with more than $1.5 billion in assets: Investors Overseas Service.

Vesco initiated dozens of dubious transactions among various entities he secretly controlled, spread across Geneva, Switzerland and the Bahamas, the Netherlands Antilles, the UK, Canada, and his home turf of New Jersey—inevitably converting investor assets for his own personal use.

In the Special Counsel report, my father seems especially irked that Vesco used ICC funds to buy a Boeing 707 jetliner for $2.3 million for his personal use. Vesco spent $600,000 sprucing it up. As David Butowsky tartly notes in his report:

"ICC clearly had no valid business purpose for acquiring the 707; its acquisition was made at Vesco's whim and for his pleasure... The renovations to the 707 rendered it commercially useless by decreasing its capacity to 33 seats. They included a discotheque area with a wooden dance floor, a bar and 'entertainment center' (including a stereo receiver, tape deck, rhythmic lighting, a wine rack and a movie screen and projector); a master bedroom; a sauna and soaking bath and shower facility."

That same pimped-out 707 would carry Robert Vesco to Costa Rica when he fled the US in early 1973. Some years later, federal agents would seize the jetliner. Undeterred, Vesco, in exile, attempted using a Panamanian shell corporation to buy back his plane. Ballsy. Later, Elvis Presley agreed to buy the 707 for $1.5 million. In response, Vesco's shell company threatened Elvis, telling him it would seize the plane; when the King reneged on the deal, one of the parties involved sued him for it.

Eventually, my father tracked Vesco to the Bahamas and one of only two hotels on Paradise Island. Dad brought me with him on one trip to meet Vesco and interview him some more. One day we are waiting in the hotel lobby, near the craps tables, and Vesco strolls right up to us and says with a convivial air, "Hello David..."

That is when I met Robert Vesco for the first time. As a boy watching him and my father give each other the business, it seemed that they kind of liked each other.

In later trips to the Bahamas, we would visit with the fugitive from US justice. In my memory, at least, we played a lot of craps. At one point my father triumphantly succeeded in seizing Vesco's 400-foot-long yacht, with its own mini submarine and helicopter. I still have the family photos of all of us standing in front of it and smiling, as if this vessel belonged to us.

Vesco had managed to buy the million-dollar yacht even while he was a fugitive from justice. He had named it for his wife: Patricia III. At one point it was seized by US Customs in Miami, and in July 1975 it was mysteriously stolen while docked for repairs. Magically it ended up in the Bahamas, where my dad hoped to re-seize it.

The seizure was short-lived. A day later the yacht disappeared, taken away by Bahamian authorities. As my dad recounts: "Special Counsel gave chase to the yacht, and this Court entered an order... requesting the cooperation of the Bahamian court, but the yacht was moved again to Panama." There, it underwent three name changes and became owned by someone who was discovered to be a Vesco associate.

Report: "The seizure, retention and subsequent loss of the Yacht Patricia III is another example of the steps which Vesco has taken to retain property obtained illegally."

Ultimately, Vesco landed in Cuba in 1982, where he was sentenced to thirteen years in prison after being accused of defrauding Fidel Castro's government by getting it to invest in a "wonder drug." He was released in 2005 and is said to have died of lung cancer in 2007, though Cuban authorities never officially reported it.

\* \* \*

While the Vesco case was my father's most famous, he may have played a far more important role in another matter. In advising independent directors of mutual funds, he helped design and institute a new rule regarding the creation of Class B shares in mutual funds, a more accessible way in for small investors. This dramatically lowered investor fees, from a stiff 5 percent at the time to what is comparatively pennies today. It would help create the current mutual-fund industry, a booming business with $16 trillion in Americans' nest eggs.

We lived in Chappaqua, New York. In high school I was a jock, playing halfback on the football team (albeit nowadays I have the build of an offensive lineman). From the start, I had an affinity for the underdog, which I trace to a lesson in the third grade when my teacher, Mr. Ferris, taught us the meaning of the word empathy. By the time of my senior year in high school, during the Iranian hostage crisis, it was only natural for me to come to the defense of an Iranian classmate of mine after he was beaten up at our school. Though I hadn't known him, I visited him at the hospital to reach out to him and assure him the rest of us at school cared about him, and later another friend and I visited him as he recuperated at home. This small gesture was deemed a big enough deal at the time to garner a story in the local newspaper, in which I was quoted as also forgiving the American kid who assaulted my new Iranian friend, because "everybody makes mistakes." Headline: "Give these students an 'A' for good will."

I graduated high school in 1980 and started out at Ithaca College in New York, playing tailback on the football team, which had been Division III national champion the previous year. My sharpest recollection is our loss to Dayton University on national television, 63–0.

After my freshman year, I moved to Texas for love, or what at the time I thought was love.

My fair-haired high school girlfriend, whom I planned to marry, had headed off to Southern Methodist University in Dallas. Her father had sent her there, I was sure, in hopes of prying us apart; it was a wise move for a daughter's father to make, and one I would make, too. Given my ornery nature at the time, however, his tactic may have made me all the more determined to pursue her.

So I made my way to Dallas, planning to surprise her by showing up unannounced at her dormitory, like Dustin Hoffman in some scene out of *The Graduate*. Late one fateful night, I got to her dorm, suitcase in hand, and discovered a note she had tacked to her front door instructing her dorm mates what to say if I should call: "If Ed calls, tell him I am at library." Meanwhile, she would be out with someone named Pete.

Pete? Who the hell was *Pete*? My heart sank right out of my rib cage, I felt sick to my stomach, and I stumbled out into the night and started hitchhiking. I was devastated, it was the first emotionally crushing experience of my young life, and in my instant reaction of fight or flight, I picked flight. When the first driver picked me up, I got in his car and made a simple request: "Please take me to the airport."

The driver did...it's just that he dropped me at the wrong one. I was unaware there were two airports in Dallas, an international airport that could let me fly to hundreds of different places and a local outlet known as Love Field, with flights to smaller markets like Austin and Little Rock, Arkansas. I was at Love Field.

The only departing flight was to Austin, so I got on it, with no idea of what I would find. Instantly I fell in love with the city and decided to transfer from Ithaca College to the University of Texas (UT), figuring it was close enough to allow me to drive over to see my high school sweetheart in Dallas, Pete notwithstanding.

A lot of guys might have bailed rather than move closer to the high school sweetie who had just crushed them. Plus, I was a Jewish outsider in Texas, a land of bible-thumping Christians; I felt self-conscious and would avoid mentioning my faith until people got to know me better.

Years later, my father would tell me that one of the most difficult things about being my dad was his being constantly surprised and puzzled by my unorthodox and unexpected reactions to situations that seemed to have only one appropriate response. It is my way to choose the road less traveled, and I am especially dogged in my determination to attain something once I set my sights on it.

## 'A Girl Like That'

Sometimes, however, in pursuit of one thing, you set your sights on something better. I was in my sophomore year at UT in Austin, still visiting my girlfriend in Dallas on weekends, when I met the true love of my life, the woman I would marry and stay partners with right up to these very days. Her name is Dani, and upon meeting her, I was thunderstruck.

Instantly I was reminded of a trip I took with my father when I was fourteen years old, to attend a UCLA basketball game. From the bleachers, we spied an inordinately lovely, beaming blonde cheerleader, vivacious and teeming with life. "Son," my dad told me as we admired her from afar, "you ever meet a girl like that, you bring her home."

Dani was "a girl like that," and she danced at basketball games as a member of the Texas Stars at UT. We met cute. On Christmas break in New York, I left a day earlier than planned and, to get home to Texas, had to take a connecting flight to Atlanta, which I never had done before. At the Atlanta airport, awaiting the final leg home to Austin, there she was, seated near the gate and waiting for the same flight. A stunner. I approached her and asked her if she would watch my bag for me for a moment, a brazen ruse she abided, whether or not she was aware of it.

On the flight, we played cards—she never had played "War" before, which still cracks me up—and I kept cheating by pulling the same card, over and over again, from the bottom of the deck: the ace of hearts, fittingly enough. It felt like we had the entire plane to ourselves. When I sat in the bleachers of a sparsely attended UT basketball game a few nights later to watch Dani dance, it was as if she and I were the only two people there, the rest of the world was out of focus.

We dated for nine years before finally getting married in 1991, and she has endured my company for a total of thirty-six years, as I write this. It occurs to me that the difficulties inherent in being with someone like me should guarantee her expedited entry to check in at the pearly gates of heaven when her time comes. She has earned it.

I graduated UT in 1985 and, reluctantly, left Dani behind in Austin to take an advertising job in Houston at a branch office of the storied, worldwide firm of Ogilvy & Mather. Think *Mad Men* set to an '80s soundtrack. A few months later my boss fired me and told me I didn't fit in at the firm, which was a correct call. O&M handed me two severance checks, one for $2,700, the other for $1,300. Together they were the fattest paycheck I had ever snagged and I was delighted. It felt like a raise. My thinking: "This is fantastic. Now what do I do?"

I boxed up my belongings, packed them into a small U-Haul trailer that I hooked to the back of my black standard-shift Celica, and left Houston to head back to Dani in Austin; we had been dating for five years by this time. As I got to Austin, I saw a billboard for a public-storage place: first month, any size, one dollar.

"I'm not gonna do this, am I?" I said to myself as I pulled into the place. I walked in, put down a buck for the biggest space available and moved in on the sly, setting up my sofa, fan, dresser, everything I owned. I stayed there for three months, showering at a nearby health club and staying with friends now and then and working odd jobs while I was figuring out what to do with myself.

Eventually, Dani graduated and moved back to her hometown of Houston, and I felt I had to get serious and find some traction. Recalling my dad's offer of an introduction at Morgan Stanley, I called in the favor and, soon after, found myself starting an entry-level training program in the financial district in Lower Manhattan on the seventy-third floor of the World Trade Center, Tower Two.

I loved it. This was my calling, this was something I could be good at doing. I spent my nights in what amounted to Jewish homelessness, crashing on my cousin's couch for a few months as I studied for the stockbroker's test, a difficult and complicated challenge known as the

Series 7 exam. All brokers must pass it to get a license to trade stocks for clients. Fail it as a trainee and you will be fired.

Morgan Stanley had an extra catch: if you pass the Series 7, you must work in the office in which you had trained for the exam; if you fail the Series 7, we fire you and you cannot get rehired. So I realized that if I passed, Morgan Stanley would keep me in New York, near my father but far away from my sweetie. Dani and I had agreed we wanted to live together in Dallas; she didn't want to live in New York. What to do?

I decided to take a dive—setting out to intentionally *fail* the Series 7. The test posed 250 questions, 125 in the morning followed by a break and then 125 questions in the afternoon. In the second session I never even looked at the questions, filling in the answer bubbles with my No. 2 pencil in an arbitrary, random pattern.

Yet I damn near passed the thing anyway. You needed 70 percent to pass, I got 67 percent.

Great story, right? Also disturbing: I almost passed the seminal Series 7 exam, which would have let me become a licensed broker, *even though I didn't even look at any of the questions* for the entire second half of the test.

My father never knew any of this, because I made sure never to tell him; it would have made him angry for various reasons, and I think he might have appreciated my effort to spare us the clash over it. He passed away in 2003.

Morgan Stanley fired me, I returned to Dallas and Dani, and soon afterward, I called the Dallas office of Morgan Stanley, looking for work. A brazen move, now that I look back on it. I was well aware of the Morgan rule.

After getting through to the branch manager at the time, Alan Schroder, I told him in unflinching fashion that I had lost out on a Morgan job in New York after taking the Series 7 and failing it on purpose. He chided me: "That's not a good thing to tell people. The branch manager in New York spent a lot of money training you, and you wasted it."

## 'Here's the Deal'

Me: "I can see that. Here's the deal: You hire me, and I'll be the best broker you ever hired. I will do everything you say and exactly what you tell me to do. Nobody works harder than I do." Happily for me, he was intrigued enough to tell me he would "go to the region and ask for this," essentially seeking approval to break the rules and rehire me. A few weeks later he brought me onboard.

The first few months I spent studying and passing the Series 7 and learning about Morgan Stanley products and processes, and my first day as a full-fledged broker came on the day after the terrifying stock plunge of Black Monday in October 1987. *The Wall Street Journal* would later dub it "Terrible Tuesday," as the world's giant banks and governments scrambled to avoid a global liquidity crisis that threatened to freeze markets and create more panic resulting in a new round of plunging stock prices.

Now you might think that would be terrible timing, but it actually was propitious. When stocks are rising and all is hunky-dory, nobody wants to take a broker's call, especially not a cold call with a sales pitch. After a market panic and a big crash, wealthy clients with money at risk are keen to hear from advisers. They seek protection, and they listen harder to what an adviser has to say.

The aftermath of Black Monday was a great time to be shopping stocks, mutual funds, and other investments to shell-shocked investors. It felt like everybody wanted to talk to me. This enabled me to deliver on all of my promises to the branch manager and then some. All I can remember is that I never stopped working, and I made sure to work harder than everyone else.

At Morgan Stanley, most brokers are doing well to open thirty-five accounts a year. In my first year, I opened two-hundred-six new accounts and was named a Rookie of the Year. Quickly, I learned to start cold calling by seven a.m. to reach business ballers before their secretaries arrived at work to screen me out. I would pause to work out at four p.m. when the markets closed, and then come back and resume calling from six to eight o'clock at night, eating dinner at my desk. Head home and get back at my desk and on the horn by seven a.m. again the next morning. Rinse and repeat.

After two years I was the number one broker in my office; by my third year I was the top performer in the southwest region; and seven or so years in, I was one of the top producers for Morgan Stanley nationwide, at the forefront of a vanguard of fourteen thousand salesmen.

I thrived by following, with blind faith, everything Morgan Stanley told me to do: how many prospects to call every day, what key things to say, which products to sell. I thought to myself: If they say jump higher, I jump higher; if they say run faster, I run faster. Whatever they said to do I did, exactly. They liked the cut of my jib so much that they had me making motivational speeches to brokers at Morgan Stanley conferences.

When Jack Kemp, the head of mutual fund sales at Morgan Stanley, hosted a meeting telling all of us brokers about the hot new mutual funds we could sell, we all got excited. He was committed to all of this, and we were too. We felt that rah-rah energy to get out there because we really believed we were doing good things for people.

The same exact thing was going on at every single firm.

Yet something was missing. I started to see through certain things in the industry, and it bothered me. I wasn't really managing other people's money; I was simply selling Morgan Stanley's chosen mutual funds and other products to generate fees for the firm. I was told to go out and sell three mutual funds: Dividend Growth, American Value, and US GVT. I didn't even know what "US GVT" was, though I later learned that it was a fund for bonds floated by the US government.

Near the end of every month, we were encouraged to make a few trades in our clients' accounts, move a few pieces around to show *action* and *active management*, just before sending out each monthly statement that would disclose our fees. The bulk of trades for Wall Street portfolios is racked up in the final week of every month or at the end of each quarter. This cynical kind of practice remains endemic to Wall Street.

Meanwhile, we lacked any defined policy aimed at ensuring the portfolios we had built for our customers were proper for their individual profiles, as defined by age, geography, cost-of-living, spending patterns, appetite for risk, resistance to losses, and so on.

Gradually it occurred to me that I had never been taught the black art of how to construct and manage a portfolio of any kind. When I asked my friends and colleagues in the business about this, they all agreed that the same lapse existed at every firm on the Street: Goldman Sachs, Merrill, UBS, all the rest. Our clients, casting aside doubt and trusting in us, clearly believed we had been trained intensively in how to invest their money, but that was and is far from the truth.

Moreover none of us had any concrete way to score how much risk each account was undertaking to achieve the returns it was targeting. This is a stunning vulnerability that afflicts all of Wall Street: we are ill-equipped to protect you from that risk, to design ways to offset it, and to let you reap new profits on it. This has been true for the last forty years, and it is still true today.

And it is a looming financial mass suicide, potentially affecting millions of investors. However wary I grew because of these factors and flaws, I kept selling, kept pursing new clients, and kept right on making money for my accounts. I opened an entirely separate office for our booming practice, serving high-end clientele, based in part on the production I was generating for the firm.

What bugs me, especially now, is that I was falling short in protecting these people. I was failing to put them into investments that would rise in value as stocks tumbled. I was leaving them inadequately prepared for the losses they might suffer due to a few changes in the economy. This unsettled me a lot, because when I tell people I will protect them, that they are safe in my hands, it obligates me to deliver on that protection. And if I am failing at it, I am failing them. I refuse to submit to that.

Worse, nobody was doing any better for their clients, and some were doing far worse. It took me another twenty years to learn better methods, to actually invent a new system for evaluating your adviser's recommendations, while quantifying and evaluating your portfolio's risk level and its abilities to deliver high enough returns to cover your true increase in the cost of living.

## Two Decades of Insights

Twenty years is a long time, especially on Wall Street. You get the benefit of my hard-won, hardheaded struggles—the CHIP Score—just by reading this book.

My father, intimately familiar with the psyche and psychology of Wall Street types, may have detected my growing sense of disillusionment. We stayed in touch as my tenure grew at Morgan Stanley. At some point during my first decade in the business, I had earned enough respect from him that he handed me a small portion of his retirement account to invest for him. I was proud to double his $12,000 in short order, although he couldn't tap the cash until after age seventy.

"Well, son," he told me on one of our periodic phone calls, "I'm so happy you doubled $12,000 to $24,000." (Beat.) "But I'll be dead before I'll ever get a chance to use it."

Now this stung hard at the time. And, once again, only later did I realize the real picture. Dad was making a joke, teasing me and urging me to keep proving myself to him, even doing so at his own expense, knowing he would likely be leaving this earth long before I would. Now that I look back on it, it was a funny line.

Like I said, life is poorly organized.

## CHAPTER 2

# Growing Disillusionment

"Hey, do you have a bill?"

Those were the first words from a guy I met as we stood in the Dallas offices of Morgan Stanley in 1996, almost a decade into my time at the world-class, white-shoe firm.

By that point I was the bona fide star of the entire Southwest region. This guy, however, was so much more. He was a Master of the Universe, descending on us from Morgan's New York headquarters. Dan Waters carried himself like a champion thoroughbred, held an MBA from Harvard,. And was laser-focused on winning.

I had 800 clients who had entrusted a combined $160 million to me by this time, and I was feeling pretty proud of myself. When I got the chance to introduce myself to him though, he asked me: "Hey, do you have a bill?"

"Sure," I said, reaching for my wallet and taking out a single dollar bill that I then handed to him. "No, you idiot! A billion under management," he shot back. Me thinking "Go screw yourself! That was pretty insulting," but telling him, "No one has a bill." And he said, "Why don't you? Why don't you have a bill?"

I had no real answer for him except I had never even dreamed of aiming so high. As brokers our expectations were to bring in maybe one hundred million dollars to manage, yielding a million dollars per year in gross commissions and taking home $400,000 per year. That qualified as a great life. But a billion dollars? When the thoroughbred said that to me, it really hit me.

The "why not?" of it got me thinking differently: why in the world don't I have a billion dollars under management, and why is his question so offensive to me? Maybe I had been thinking too small, while other guys with half my smarts were operating on a scale ten times as large as mine, their compensation commensurate with those heights.

That lesson applied to my broader life as well, making me wonder whether I was settling for just OK and failing to challenge myself to step up and make more of an effort at *everything* in my life.

I had always been motivated less by money and more by my desire to help regular people by investing their money to allow them to reach higher levels of financial comfort and safety. One of my first clients was Burl Phelps, who stayed with me for twenty-seven years after retiring from Conoco Philips. He was able to live well thanks to his pension and a $500,000 retirement account, until he passed in 2018 at age ninety-four. I still manage the account for his family because I appreciate the faith and trust he put in me long ago.

Still, a notion began taking shape in my mind. My client roster, supposedly focused on serving individual investors, had grown so large as to be impersonal. It's not as though I had established emotional bonds with all my clients; I had signed up too many of them to be able to do that any longer. I had brokers under me handling much of the personal contact, and for most clients I didn't know the names of their children or the specifics of how they had earned their wealth, unless I checked the notes I had scribbled into their entries in my Day-Timer.

A creeping, awkward sense of embarrassment began to take hold of me, and I couldn't shake it: nobody knew whether or not we were making our clients' lives any better. This unnerved me to no end. Wall Street sells the lie that we provide individualized service, that we take care of you and we care about you, but how many people can each broker realistically know and care about and study and analyze? I figure the maximum efficient total may be, say, a few dozen. That's it. Yet by that point I had 800 clients under my watch.

## 'Who the Hell Is This Guy?'

All of this crystallized in me on one particular day a few months after the "Do you have a bill" exchange with the Morgan Stanley thoroughbred. I got a surprise call from one of my clients. His voice was gravelly and thickly Deep Texas, and he launched into his spiel without introducing himself.

Him: "Ed, I just gotta tell you what a great job you've done for me."

Me: "Well, thank you, sir," ("Who the hell is this guy?")

Him: "You did exactly what you said you would do, you put me in Florida Progress (stock), and Ed, we haven't talked at all, that darn thing's doubled!"

That was great, except at the time I was thinking about how this man believed I cared about him—and I couldn't even conjure up his name. This was in the days before caller ID, so I punched a few keys on the Quotron machine to call up my clients who had FPG in their accounts. Even once I found his name, though, I still didn't know him.

I felt like a fake, and suddenly I realized what a liar I was. These clients thought I was looking after their accounts, they believed I was concerned about them, and for well over half of them, I didn't even know who they were. Shame on me, yes, and shame on Wall Street.

I wanted to remake myself into a higher form of financial adviser, managing billions of dollars instead of millions, and imbued with a deeper knowledge of the markets and their most sophisticated secrets—think Neo in *The Matrix Reloaded*. Now the man can fly.

By this time, I was well aware of a stark difference between the conversations we brokers were having with our clients and the conversations taking place between the really high-end financial advisers and their clients. At the retail level, we were talking about mutual funds, municipal bond funds, and the like. In the higher realm of wealth management, the really smart people weren't talking about mutual funds, they were talking about collars, spreads, straddles, ratios and liquidity needs. They were speaking this sophisticated language, while I fielded calls from a retired Texan asking whether he would get his dividend payment on a Tuesday or a Thursday—he could remember only that it came on a "T" day. It felt like the rank-and-file brokers were speaking Mandarin, the most common language in China, and the high-end advisers were speaking Cantonese, the country's more exotic variant. I wanted to learn that other language.

The next morning, I set out on a drastic change of course. I did something almost no broker would do: I gave away most of my client base. I grabbed a stack of new-account cards listing contact information for my latest sign-ups and started handing them out to the pleased but puzzled brokers all around me. Ultimately, I handed off fully 70 percent of the client roster I had cultivated and tended to for almost a decade.

I even gave up my father's account, after he had ticked me off with that joke about dying before getting any chance to spend the assets that I had doubled for him. (I handed the account to a broker who had been an usher at my wedding.)

Shedding more than 500 accounts freed me up to pursue investors with accounts that were bigger, far bigger. It was exhilarating and cathartic for me, a fresh start on something entirely different. Turned on by the challenge, I started working on hauling in hundreds of millions of dollars. After two years I had my first "bill," and within four years I had collected a gargantuan eleven billion dollars, the bulk of it from half a dozen or so super-accounts.

I had entered the business a decade before as a grunt, one of thousands of entry-level brokers brought on during a hiring binge by the biggest firms to better compete in the war for billions of dollars in investors' savings. Merrill Lynch fired the first shot in the early 1980s when it hired the renowned consulting firm McKinsey & Co. to conduct a top-to-bottom strategic review with an eye toward future growth.

Wall Street had come of age as a provider of bespoke and highly sophisticated financial advice reserved for the wealthiest investors and corporations in the world. It had operated this way since its founding in 1817, and continued to do so.

McKinsey determined that Merrill should launch a full-on moonshot, hire and train thousands upon thousands of new brokers in a mad dash for new accounts and open dozens of new offices to put those new brokers as close as possible to the local investors they hoped to serve. (This was in the days before the start of online trading.)

Whether the newly minted brokers went on to make it in the business mattered far less than how many new accounts they could sign and how much new money they could collect for their firm to manage. If 25 percent flunked out every year, so be it—the accounts they opened would be left behind for the survivors.

Merrill heeded McKinsey's advice, and the other big investment banks followed suit. Suddenly a patrician business once filled with elite counselors was brimming with bravado from newcomers with lesser pedigrees who hailed from all walks of life. The big firms wanted to deploy so many people that anyone who could fog a mirror was eligible for hire. Yet quantity is the enemy of quality, as a friend of mine likes to say, quoting a message from a fortune cookie he opened years ago.

The result, inevitably, was legions of mediocre registered reps, people with no special skills or training in managing other people's money, people who were at best salesmen and who could have been selling most anything, whether stocks or stacks of sheet metal. This struck me now and again, like the time I overheard another broker in the Dallas office put the squeeze on a reluctant client who had said he wanted to confer with his wife before making a final decision—"Mr. Jackson, we're not buying drapes here. You don't have to ask your wife," the broker exhorted him.

No talk of better returns or tax advantages, just impugn the man's masculinity. It had all the subtlety of a lead-pipe cinch, and it came, fittingly, from the mouth of a broker who had worked previously as a plumber. (And yes, his name was Joe, though this was not Joe the Plumber, who found fleeting fame during Barack Obama's successful presidential run in 2008.)

With thousands of new brokers to manage, Merrill, Morgan, and the other giants needed to hire branch managers and other bosses, but where to find them? In many cases they hired from the ranks of the failed brokers who had been culled from the herd, the guys who were less aggressive, less persistent, less creative, less successful. This is the type of adviser now running a lot of branch offices for the big Wall Street firms. They mean well and believe they are doing a bang-up job, and they are delusional.

The onrush of new brokers in the late '80s and beyond was followed by a cataclysmic change in 1999: the elimination of the Glass-Steagall Act, passed during the failure of five thousand banks in the Great Depression to impose a separation between investment banking and regular banking. The repeal allowed commercial banks that take in money from the masses to take a bigger role in investing in the volatile markets.

When lawmakers lifted Glass-Steagall, the floodgates opened for new financial advisers of all sorts. Suddenly actual insurance salesmen, who had no training in finance and investing, were selling mutual funds to their customers.

Around this time, I used to spend Saturday mornings at breakfast at the Gleneagles Country Club in Plano, Texas, meeting with an insurance broker buddy. Over the previous three years we had developed a synergistic referral loop, he handed me life insurance clients so I could give them investing advice, and I handed him investing clients who wanted his insurance advice.

Then one Saturday morning, he told me: "I can't do that anymore." His insurance firm wanted him to sell mutual funds to his clients now, so he wouldn't be referring them to me. "But you don't have an idea what you're even talking about," I told him. "I know," he told me. They weren't trained in how to do it, they were just told to go out and do it, he explained.

So there were thousands of new and untrained rookies in the brokerage business, former insurance salesmen who suddenly had renamed themselves financial advisers, in an even further stretch of the truth. Title inflation, taken to the extreme.

## We Were Taught to Sell

These denizens of Wall Street might be better at doing their jobs if Wall Street were better at training them to do it. Unbeknownst to the public, the dirty little secret of wealth management is that none of us ever were taught how to set up our clients' array of assets, how to spread risk and offset it in equal measure. Portfolio construction, suitability to the client, and managing money were a mystery to us.

We were taught to sell. By selling the products our Wall Street overlords told us to sell, we believed we were doing something good for clients, never mind whether the firms' underlying motivation was to generate revenue for themselves.

I hoped the story would be different among the ranks of advisers to ultra-high-net-worth clients at Morgan Stanley. As I began courting big blue-chip clients with millions more to invest than I had ever imagined handling, I expected the whole set-up would be far superior to what I had seen as a broker on smaller accounts.

Surely, I felt, these upper-crust advisers must have conducted deeper research, considered diversified investment options, and sought out sage guidance from veterans with far more experience than I had. And surely they had smarter and safer methods for handling how much risk their clients should assume to get the returns needed to fund their retirement.

Those were my hopes. What I found were just nopes. These guys at the top of the food chain were really no better at the most important elements of investing their clients' money than the ex-plumbers and the other palookas on the phone for the big brokerage houses. No better at assessing risk and tamping it down, no better at figuring out how much money their clients really needed to keep living securely, and no better at diversifying and blending an array of assets in sensible ways.

Their biggest shortcoming, as with everyone else on Wall Street, was in managing risk. Given the lamentably lame job that most players on Wall Street do in detecting risk and coming up with ways to quantify it and neutralize it, not to mention the regulators who are supposed to be their masters, it becomes paramount that investors themselves must learn to do it.

Imagine setting up your retirement account so that it throws off enough investment income each year to cover all your expenses without your ever having to draw down the principal that you have been building up for your entire career. Designing and setting up this self-perpetuating money machine requires taking on significant risk in the right ways, hedging those bets, and offsetting them with creative and out-of-the-mainstream moves.

Before you dare take aim at that target, you must educate yourself to get better at risk identification and assessment and make yourself more comfortable with taking on the *right* amount of risk so as to maximize returns. That requires a deeper dive into learning about risk and all that it entails, and that is coming up next.

# CHAPTER 3

# Risk and Ignorance

One oft-quoted axiom of investing holds that the secret to getting rich is less a matter of the killing you make on your investments and more about the avoidance of losses along the way. Or as the legendary Benjamin Graham (1884–1976) put it in the last chapter of his renowned 1949 bible of investing, *The Intelligent Investor*: "Confronted with a challenge to distill the secret of sound investment into three words, we venture the motto, Margin of Safety." To that let us add an apt one-liner from the inimitable Oracle of Omaha, the assiduously folksy financier Warren Buffett: "Risk comes from not knowing what you're doing."

On Wall Street, the level of risk increases exponentially, for we have more investing experts than ever before, dispensing financial advice to more investors than ever before, and the vast majority of them don't know how to manage risk and the nasty surprises it can entail.

It is a startling and disturbing flaw that runs deep in even the biggest and best firms on Wall Street. This amounts to a stunning betrayal of the investor who has enough money to entrust to a financial adviser from Morgan Stanley or Goldman Sachs or any of the storied names you have heard for decades, names that evoke dollar signs and pinstripes and fancy suspenders (or braces as we called them in the roaring '90s).

The world's most revered names in investment banking are bad at detecting and deflecting risk for their clients, even clueless at times, and their lesser lights in smaller shops are even worse at it, in many cases. It is an unforgivable sin, for risk is at the very foundation of all investing; it is one of the building blocks that dictate the design, direction, and development of most everything that follows in their wake.

The seesawing balance between level-of-risk and level-of-returns is the key pivot point for all investing. If you want stellar returns that might have a chance of rising 40 percent in a year, it may require taking on immense risk that could trigger a loss of, say, 25 percent of your life's savings in a single swipe.

Most of us are risk-averse when it comes to losing money. Studies show investors are two-and-a-half times more negative about losing money on an investment than they are happy about reaping a gain. And so we invest conservatively, willingly accepting lower returns to avoid the risk of losing "bigly," as President Donald Trump would put it.

Thus, bonds issued by the US government pay lower interest rates to the bondholder than, say, utility bonds issued by a city or high-yield "junk bonds" issued by a corporation. This is because the US bonds are viewed as safer, all but guaranteed to get paid back, while local governments can stumble and default. A corporation sometimes belly flops, therefore it must offer investors higher interest rates than they can get from government bonds, to reward them for taking on the higher risk that the company might never repay them.

The risks of owning stock in a company run even higher, thus stocks must promise an extra upside in terms of a rising price or a dividend that exceeds the yield on a bond. Bond yields always exceeded dividend yields on stocks until about ten years ago, when they crossed over and stocks' dividends rose higher than bond interest rates. Most stocks prefer growth over dividends, though, and that is the main reason to invest in stocks—for capital growth.

In a corporate meltdown, the company's equity—the stock owned by shareholders in the firm—can get wiped out as the stock price falls to zero (as happens when companies file for reorganization under Chapter 11 of the federal bankruptcy code). A total loss. Debt-holders, by contrast, are first in line to get paid as bankers sell off assets to raise money to repay bonds before deigning to meet any other obligations. Lenders come first, always; owners come last. It has been this way for centuries of commerce.

Art imitates life, the old saying goes, and so does investing. Just as you take bigger risks when you are younger and feel like you will live forever—and don't know any better—so can you take bigger investment risks when you are younger and have years to make up any momentary swoon in the markets. Put another way, just as you end up taking fewer risks on the ski slopes when you have passed a certain age and your joints can't take the pounding they once endured painlessly, so must you reduce the risks you take in investing as you get older and your time shortens for recovering from losses.

Wall Street advisers, in evaluating their own performance on your behalf, often cite only one key question: how much did the total combined value of your assets rise in the previous three months? It is a terrible question, because it is the *wrong* question.

You can have the highest returns in investing history, but that means nothing in the bigger picture. That's because performance means nothing—and I mean nothing—unless it is evaluated in the context of *risk*. In a strong, robust market, as the old cliché has it, a rising tide lifts all boats. When everybody's up, the question becomes how much risk did you have to take on in your portfolio to reap those rewards? How much protection did you have in place? How much in fees and costs did you have to cover? How much of your gains did you have to pay in taxes?

And I'm talking over a period of ten or twenty or thirty years, not just one quarter; that's what counts. Wall Street wealth managers barely speak in these terms because most don't know they should be doing so, and those who do know don't care.

## Broken Portfolios

One can argue that fully 97.5 percent of all investment portfolios managed by Wall Street—we are talking trillions of dollars—are broken or inefficient and fail to measure up to investors' needs. This is because 97.5 percent of portfolios lack alternative investments (hedge funds, options, futures, precious metals, diamonds, luxury automobiles, perhaps even such exotica as baseball cards—up 17 percent a year over the past few decades). Without alternatives, it is all but impossible to significantly reduce the downside risk in a portfolio.

When you invest, you should first have a sense of how much downside you can handle in a twelve-month period. Say you invested a million dollars and by year-end it had lost $100,000. Most people would say that is as much downside risk as they could handle.

That is just a 10 percent dip over an entire year. Most investment portfolios at the Wall Street giants have a downside-to-upside range of –25 percent to +40 percent—that is, most portfolios have as much chance of falling 25 percent in a year as they do of rising 40 percent in a year, with the vast majority of accounts finishing up somewhere in between. Most financial advisers are unaware that their own model portfolios include this flawed proclivity for volatility.

If you are lucky, your returns might at least match those of the broad stock indexes such the Dow and the S&P 500. If you are lucky. The fact is most active fund managers, who trade in and out of stocks and other assets, endeavoring to outfox the rest of the market, trail the broad indexes over the long term.

Wise long-term investing requires a counterintuitive mix of unrelenting optimism and constant caution. Instead of thinking about how much money you will make in the next twelve months, which is what your broker wants you to focus on, you should be thinking about *the probability of loss* in the next twelve months. Your adviser should be talking to you about the worst that could happen and what that would mean in dollars and percentage.

Probabilities are what matters when assessing risk. In order to have the freedom to live the way you want, you must understand risk. That's also true of the people who are supposed to be taking care of your life savings. Instead, you are beholden to people who don't ask these questions, who don't understand capital risk or other kinds of risk; they don't tell you that you might lose 18 percent this year and another 19 percent next year.

At one point in my investing career, I had a good chat with a client named Cliff, and I asked him, "If you looked at your portfolio and suddenly it was down by $200,000, how would you feel?" Him: "I wouldn't be able to sleep." Yet he had an account topping ten million dollars, so I told him: "Okay, Cliff, that means you can't handle being down 2 percent...so how do you expect me to get you 10 percent returns in a year if you can't handle being down only 2 percent?" He never had thought of it that way.

No risk, no reward. No pain, no gain. You get that, right? Everybody does, in theory.

Suppose someone offers you a million dollars to walk a tightrope. You think, "Wow, that would be great! A million dollars just to walk a tightrope!" Think of that as being solely focused on *performance*. All you have to do is make it across and you win. Most money managers think this way. All they have to do is make is to the end of the quarter with a return that beats the market, and they win.

Except the next thing that comes to your mind is, "Wait, how high off the ground is that tightrope?" That's where risk comes into play. If the tightrope were a thousand feet off the ground, then you would be taking a gigantic risk—your life—to earn that million-dollar return. That is not the kind of portfolio you want your broker to construct, because if there is a lot of risk and its value falls precipitously, you could lose it all, just like falling off that tightrope.

Now suppose that tightrope is one foot off the ground. Then the deal is a no-brainer. That's a risk you would take every time. It also is something that never would happen, because nobody will give you a million dollars to walk a tightrope one foot off the ground. They might give you ten bucks, but you can't get something for nothing.

So let's apply this to investing. If I told you I could design your portfolio so it had as much chance of returning up to 20 percent a year as it did of losing up to 25 percent in a year, would you take that chance? You should instantly know the answer is "No way."

This is how brokers and financial managers should be phrasing their questions, because this is what risk is all about. Investors get blinded by the potential upside. Say you visit two portfolio managers: The first can construct a portfolio that (based on past performance) could lose 20 percent in a year or rise as much as 40 percent, staying within that range 95 percent of the time. The second can construct a portfolio, with the same 95 percent consistency, that has a range of 6 percent to 14 percent a year. Which would you choose?

You should choose the second manager every time. I would rather have a high probability that even in my worst year I would still make money (6 percent), and in my very best year I'd beat the historical average of 10 percent by earning 14 percent. That's because there is a very low probability (only 5 percent of the time in the past) that I would do worse, or even lose money. I gladly would forfeit any chance of earning 40 percent to avoid risking a loss of 20–25 percent in a year. So should you, by the way.

Let's break it down further, starting with your imaginary one-million-dollar portfolio. Suppose the first money manager you visited does great this year and earns 40 percent on your portfolio. At the end of the year you have $1.4 million. The second year, however, he loses 20 percent, and you are down to $1.12 million. Meanwhile, let's say the second manager hits his top target of a 14 percent return on your portfolio in year one, and the next year hits his downside low of 6 percent. You would end up with $1.224 million, which is 9 percent better than the first manager achieved in his two years.

Who would you choose now? Which manager's portfolio would let you sleep better at night and feel better enduring high-volatility days?

Risk is a critical factor when constructing a portfolio because it is an emotional part of our lives. When things get bad, we tend to believe those bad times will continue. We imagine what will happen if things fail to improve. That's why you see people selling at the bottom, they get so afraid of losing even more than they have lost already that they sell out in a panic.

Yet when things are going great and the market is way up, we don't think about preserving our gains. We don't even consider selling. It's as if we are at a craps table in Vegas, we're on a heater, and we want our investments to keep running! Our emotions get the better of us. That's always been true. Emotion creates volatility, which creates risk. The more emotional we get as investors, the more likely we are to buy or sell on a whim, which increases everyone's risk.

CNBC, Fox Business, and all the twenty-four-hour news channels are continually trying to generate emotion, to get people to act. In a market meltdown that can do a disservice to all investors, who are better off if they can learn to neutralize the natural, knee-jerk reactions to the careening highs and lows that can accompany investing.

## Anticipation is Preparation

Anticipation is preparation. If you know the kinds of risk that can threaten your portfolio and require you to respond urgently to sidestep the consequences, you are one step ahead of most of the pack. And like the old joke about two pals getting chased by a hungry bear, you don't have to outrun the bear (market), only the other guy, by beating him in the race to an undervalued safe haven.

Most investors think of risk in a fairly simple way: stocks are risky, bonds less so, and they might lose money that they invest in either one. That's about the extent of it. Most brokers and money managers don't bother to educate clients about the different types of risk that exist with different kinds of investments.

To truly invest successfully you have to understand all the risks that are out there. Your money manager must be able to discuss these risks with you and explain *how to quantify them*. Keep reading and you won't need them anymore, you will learn to do it yourself. By my count, essentially eight categories of risk loom over investing, and you must be aware of each and every one of them.

## Risk #1: Inflation Risk

This is the risk of erosion in your purchasing power. It is the most insidious, damaging risk of all and the one that is hardest to predict. If your retirement account is growing 3 percent a year and your food and housing costs are rising 12 percent a year, you are losing purchasing power at a desperate rate.

Government statistics show that inflation has been rising at 2 percent or less a year for several years. In many parts of America, the cost of living is rising much faster than that. As we will see later, government statistics intentionally understate the real rise in the cost of living so as to reduce the COLA payments that Social Security must cover to keep pace with the official inflation rate. It amounts to a premeditated mass deception, and the implications of this understatement of the real rise in prices in your daily life are devastating. You first must get a grip on the real inflation in your life, how much the costs of your daily activities are increasing each year, before you can assess whether your portfolio is producing the returns you require to preserve your purchasing power.

If you fail to do this, you could be one of the millions of people who commit a long, slow financial suicide, and they don't even know it.

## Risk 2: Capital Risk

This is the risk that the investments you bought will decrease in value from the prices you paid, causing you to lose money if you end up having to sell at the lower prices. In past financial crises, investors who panicked and sold at the bottom locked in their losses, even though asset values eventually rebounded and rose from there. Capital risk is twofold, actually: the first risk is that your asset value declines; the second is that you react unwisely out of fear and make the losses permanent.

## Risk #3: Correlation Risk

You may have heard that diversification of your portfolio is a good thing. This is because it helps you avoid *correlation risk*—or putting too many of your investment eggs in too few, or too similar, baskets. The challenge in today's global economy is finding truly non-correlated assets that operate oppositely to the main elements of your portfolio. While twenty years ago you could offset the risk of a plunge in US stocks by buying stocks in major markets overseas or even in smaller emerging markets more recently, today stocks trade in tandem across all of those markets. They all are correlated to one another, and you must search harder to find truly non-correlated, against-the-grain hedges for your account.

## Risk #4: Liquidity Risk

This is the risk that you may be unable to convert your investment into cash if you need to raise capital fast. It exists mainly in private equity investments, real estate, venture capital, and some securities that rarely trade. When it comes to things like collectibles, antiques, diamonds or exotic investments, you may be unable to sell them at all, just when you need to do so....

**Risk #5: Horizon Risk**

This is a tricky category that can elude even a skilled wealth manager. When you invest your savings, you should plan on at least a ten-year window or time horizon. Markets (and the wealth they create) grow in jagged patterns, with plenty of ups and plenty of downs. Your investments will need time to recover from losses, and if you can wait long enough, most of the time they will. Over the truly long term, in a century or more of trading on the NYSE, stocks rose an average of 6 percent a year, despite down years and bear markets and cataclysmic crashes.

What happens, though, if an emergency necessitates you sell after only one year rather than waiting a decade for your investment to mature? Say you lose your job. Or incur a huge medical expense not covered by insurance—if you even carry health insurance. You have to sell, but what if the market crashed four months earlier and your investments are down 30 percent? You sell and take the loss.

The best way to handle horizon risk is to invest no more than you can afford to lose. It is a striking contradiction: hoping to build wealth by using cash you can afford to burn. Here is another one: a longer time horizon in investing is a means to reduce risk, yet for bondholders the longer horizon *increases* risk.

If you own an old government bond paying 2 percent a year, and new bonds of the same duration are paying 5 percent, you are losing out in a major way. This is why a thirty-year government bond must pay a higher interest rate than, say, a two-year government bond. You take on much higher risk by locking up your money for such a long period of time because you are unable to shift it to safer grounds in the event of market disruptions, global panics, recessions, and other forms of hell that can break loose at any time.

When investors use a bond ladder to invest in a revolving array of bonds that mature at various times—short-term, every six months; medium-term, every ten years; long-term, every thirty years—they are managing horizon risk.

### Risk #6: Currency Risk

More than half the profits of most multinational corporations these days are generated overseas. So, even though you think you don't have any international investments, you do if you own the stock of a company that does business overseas or you own mutual funds that own such stocks. When the US dollar rises in value against rival currencies such as the euro or the British pound, it can hurt the dollar earnings of US titans back home.

Starbucks is Seattle-based but has thousands of stores abroad, with transactions conducted in local currencies. Buy a coffee at a Starbucks in Berlin and you will pay in euros. In Budapest, you'll pay in Hungarian forint. When Starbucks adds up all its revenue from other countries, using the currency of that country, it then has to convert the total into dollars.

If the value of a local currency declines in relation to the US dollar over a certain period of time, then when that local currency is converted back into dollars, the reported revenue and any associated profits will be lower than they otherwise would have been. Lower profits can lead to lower stock prices, because stock prices almost always follow earnings.

I say almost always because of exceptions that prove the rule, such as Amazon, whose stock has soared over the past decade even as the company's earnings have often been nonexistent or eaten away by massive expansion projects and discount pricing. In the decade prior to March 2018, Amazon's earnings rose less than sixfold, yet its stock price rose almost twentyfold.

### Risk #7: Credit Risk

This is the risk every lender and bond buyer must contemplate when putting their cash on the table: what happens if I don't get paid back? This is what's known as credit risk, the risk that the credit extended to the company never gets repaid. So if you have invested in company debt of some sort, you have to evaluate the credit risk of each and every investment you make.

Standard & Poor's, Fitch Group, and Moody's Investor Service all built billion-dollar businesses by issuing credit ratings for corporate bond issues, local governments, and other concerns which assessed the likelihood that investors would be paid back without a problem.

Fitch's ratings, for example, start at a high of AAA, for large, financially strong companies likely to withstand any foreseeable event, then move down a notch to AA, for those with a very low default risk, and so on, all the way down to the worst of the worst—or rather the riskiest of the risky—the lowly C, for companies in which the "default or default-like process has begun, or the issuer is in standstill."

## Risk #8: Longevity Risk

Bluntly stated, this is the risk that you outlive your savings. The longer you are alive, the greater the chance that you will run out of money. Retired investors who are earning a real rate of return that fails to keep up with the real increases in their personal cost of living, and who have no other regular income or savings, could run out of money before they die.

It is doubtful that the government's Social Security program will make up the difference for many people. When Social Security payments commenced in 1940, the government promise was that payments would start at age sixty-five and continue for the rest of the recipient's life. But life expectancy was sixty-one for men and sixty-five for women. Just nine million people were age sixty-five or older in 1950.

Today the average life expectancy in America is seventy-six for men, eighty-one for women, meaning payments must last for ten to fifteen years longer. Plus some fifty million Americans are sixty-five or older. Every single day, another ten thousand baby boomers turn sixty-five and start receiving Social Security.

The financial consequences of this influx are overwhelming and devastating. Worse, back when the Social Security program began, the US had six workers paying into the retirement fund on behalf of every one retiree; today it is almost fewer than *three* workers for each retiree. The burden-per-worker has doubled, even as the government obligation has dramatically increased.

The center will not hold. Social Security will go bankrupt or suffer massive cuts in payouts. You should assume the program will die before you do—and brace yourself to do without it. You may want to forget Social Security income altogether and make plans for your own financial future, because in the end it will all be up to you.

* * *

So many forms of risk exist, so many things that could come between you and your money. Add them all up, considering different variations at different points in time, and you have the range of possibilities for your portfolio. Calculating the range of possible outcomes based on past results is crucial to your investment planning. Narrow that range and you cut down on volatility in your account. In the following chapter, you will learn more about how to do this. It entails getting comfortable with a nerdy, daunting mathematical term known as standard deviation.

# CHAPTER 4

# Deviant Behavior

An awful lot of time could be wasted trying to come up with an inventive entry to the complex topic known as standard deviation. So, let's go with the provocatively skewed title above and just cut to it.

Reading those two words, standard deviation, may make you wince, but this will be more compelling than the boring statistics class you had in college, because we are talking about how to get rich. Understanding standard deviation can help you comprehend risk and let you quantify it in your portfolio, allowing you to determine whether you are taking on too much of it. Even better, standard deviation can help you quantify just how much money you could lose in a given year, in stark dollar terms.

Your gains always must be weighed against the risk of wealth destruction that you willingly, or unknowingly, took on to attain those returns. The question "What were your returns over such-and-such period of time?" means nothing in a vacuum. You can have the highest returns in investing history, but performance means nothing—and I mean nothing—unless it is evaluated in the context of risk.

Few financial advisers know much about standard deviation, and even fewer talk to their clients about it. Given the many failures of Wall Street advisers regarding risk, the individual investor must understand standard deviation better, and this requires knowing the ins and outs of the term. Your familiarity with it will help you have a clearer conversation with your adviser about the biggest risks in your portfolio.

In Chapter Three we talked about risk and offered an example of two advisers with different approaches. One adviser offers an average return of 10 percent a year with a 95 percent chance that your account's range of volatility runs from up 40 percent to down 20 percent. While actual results will fall somewhere in this range, you have just as good a chance in any given year of making 40 percent as you do of *losing* 20 percent.

Nobody should be comfortable with that high level of risk.

The other adviser we mentioned offers you a 95 percent chance at returns that have a maximum upside of only 14 percent for any given year and a downside of still being up 6 percent. A much safer bet. Though we didn't tell you at the time—it was too early—those numbers arise from different *standard deviations* for the two portfolios.

Technically, standard deviation, or STD in Wall Street's unfortunate abbreviation for the term, describes how much one particular set of data has deviated in the past from the average of the larger data set that encompasses it. For investing purposes, standard deviation is a way of placing a number on how much risk and volatility your portfolio (and your nerves) sustained in reaping its returns.

Boiled down, standard deviation is a volatility index, and the higher the STD, the higher the volatility, and consequently the wider the range of ups and downs your portfolio has gone through in the previous ten-year period. You want your portfolio to churn out high returns while also having a narrower range of possible outcomes and a reduced chance of downside losses. So, you should seek as low a standard deviation as possible for your overall account.

A standard deviation of zero would be perfect: say you could earn 10 percent a year for ten years without any change up or down in any year, no volatility, zero deviation from the norm, zero risk, zero worry.

This reminds me of the comedian Chris Rock's bit about marriage: "If you're in a good relationship, chances are you are bored out of your [effin'] mind. All good relationships are boring; the only exciting relationships are bad ones. You never know what's going to happen tomorrow when you're in a bad relationship."

Investing is like that, too: the slower and steadier and more boring, the better. This is why the assets I manage have a turnover rate of only 5 percent in a year; stand down and wait, and always be watching.

By quantifying this risk and volatility as the standard deviation, based on results over a long period of time, you will have a better sense of where your investments have been and where they most likely are headed. At the least, you can better anticipate the possible range of outcomes, because they have occurred 95 percent of the time in the previous decade or more. The hope is that the next year might be much like the ten years leading up to it.

Let's say your portfolio posted an average annual return of 8 percent over the previous ten years. Standard deviation entails measuring how far away from that average your returns strayed in those ten years, during any individual month and over the entire 120 months—how much higher *and* how much lower. The high and the low set the outer boundaries for how widely your returns varied—how drastically they deviated from the mean, the average 8 percent return each year for the previous decade.

Put another way, how much *volatility* did you have to endure to reap the average growth rate your portfolio produced? Lower volatility equals a lower standard deviation, and that means a smoother path to higher returns. Think of your portfolio as the ultimate streamlined Olympic bobsled, one that travels farther and faster by hewing to the perfect line and avoiding inefficient swerves back and forth.

## Quantifying Risk

For most of this book I have carped at Wall Street for its inability to identify and manage risk and, especially, to quantify it. Well, standard deviation is a great way to quantify risk, although that is just the first step to devising a better way to construct your portfolio. Here are some examples to illustrate it, because this is easier to understand than it appears.

Say your 401(k) had a rate of return of 8 percent a year for the past ten years, based on the average returns of your entire account in that full decade. Now, in one year your account managed a stellar 18 percent return, but in another year it hit the worst return it would produce, down 2 percent. This is oversimplified, but go with me here. This would mean your account had a (first) standard deviation of ten. That is to say, the best it did was ten percentage points higher than the average return of 8 percent (that stellar 18 percent return in one particular year), and the worst it performed was ten percentage points below the average 8 percent return (-2 percent or down 2 percent in a year).

In that case, was it worth risking the worst downside of being down 2 percent in any given year to have a pretty sure bet on 8 percent annual returns? It might have been.

Many portfolios on Wall Street, however, are set up like the one offered by our first adviser, meaning a 10 percent average annual return requires a willingness to risk a 20 percent loss in a single year with the maximum potential gain of 40 percent. That choice is more obvious— risking a loss in any year that is double your average annual gain isn't worth the promise of the average return (which was 10 percent). Yet it is done all the time, often without anyone knowing they are doing it, neither the investor nor their paid adviser.

Given the old adage of no risk no reward, the higher your rate of return over the previous ten years, the higher your account's standard deviation is likely to be. You had to endure that wider range of what could go wrong and assume that higher risk, in order to attain those lofty heights.

Here is an important guardrail: *the standard deviation for your portfolio should be no higher than 80 percent of your average annual return*. So, for an account with an average annual return of 10 percent over the past ten years, the standard deviation should be eight or lower. Thanks to math we will explain further down, it means the steepest loss you endured in the previous ten years was down 6 percent in a year. Survivable.

If your account had a standard deviation of fifteen to get that 10 percent return, it would equate to 150 percent of your return rate, almost double the 80 percent level (or lower) that I recommend, and that is way too much risk. In other words you could have lost 20 percent in a single year, and that could happen two years in a row. Deadly.

Knowing more about standard deviation has a secondary benefit: you can learn a lot about your financial advisers by asking them about it. If he or she has no idea what the metric is and doesn't use it, find another financial adviser. If they do know about standard deviation, it opens up the conversation to the moves your adviser has taken and the moves that should be made in the future.

You can start the conversation by asking your broker: if my account has an average annual rate of return of 10 percent in the past ten years, what should be its standard deviation to have gotten that return? As we just said, eight is the right answer (80 percent of the average annual rate of return), but almost every broker will say fifteen, because the only standard deviation they know is that of the stock market. That is way too high.

Measuring your portfolio's standard deviation can help you assess its risks and vulnerabilities and reconstruct it to better pursue your goals, shedding some assets and adding others. Once you know the STD of your investment account over the past ten years, you can focus on the real game: getting a solid, sufficient average annual return on your portfolio over the long term while reducing the risk and volatility it takes to get there. You can apply the stencil of standard deviation to every investment in your portfolio, mixing and matching and blending all these varying standard deviations to come up with as low a number as possible for your account overall.

Your adviser or the company that holds your account should be able to compute the STD for you, or check the company website. Ten years should be the minimum timespan for measuring rate of return in your portfolio and the standard deviation underlying it; twenty years is even better. It is a waste of time to look at anything less, and all but meaningless in divining a real trend.

One of the shrewdest investors of the past twenty years is the controversial hedge fund manager Steven Cohen, whose former firm SAC Capital consistently posted some of the highest returns in the industry. Even more impressive, he landed these extraordinary returns while tamping down the volatility and risk of his investments. (These investments often were alternatives, as a hedge fund's *raison d'etre* is to go against the grain and provide a hedge against downward swings in the markets for stocks and/or bonds).

Cohen posted a 25 percent average annual rate of return for the previous ten or twenty years, with an unusually low standard deviation of only 8. This means he produced rich returns while maintaining low volatility and a narrow range of investment outcomes. Recall that an STD should be at only 80 percent of your average rate of return or even lower, so in Cohen's case that would be an STD of 20, yet his funds had an 8, at only 32 percent of his annual return. Extraordinary.

Now, here is the math behind Cohen's standard deviation of 8 and what it means. Basically, you take Cohen's average return of 25 percent and add the STD of 8 to it to get one standard deviation: 25% + 8 = 33%. This means that, with 70 percent probability, the highest the fund will return will be 33 percent in any given twelve-month period. To get to 95 percent probability you must add a second standard deviation:

$$25\% + 8 + 8 = 41\%.$$

This means that, 95 percent of the time in the past, Cohen's funds had an average annual return of 25 percent with a maximum upside of as much as 41 percent. Now, to compute the downside risk, you *subtract* the STD from the average rate of return, and you do so a second time to get to the second standard deviation and "95 percent of the time" certainty:

$$25\% - 8 - 8 = +9\%.$$

Thus, 95 percent of the time in the past, Cohen funds had at worst a downside of +9%.

That is an awesome track record—invest for ten years with the downside being at worst an average gain of 9 percent per year; at a return of 10 percent per year your assets *double* in value in only 7.2 years. For these rich returns, Cohen charged some of the highest fees in the business—3 percent of assets plus a 30 percent cut of any profits his funds earned in a year. Even so, wouldn't you pay a fee of "three and thirty" to get in on such a safe bet that offers such a strong return?

## Too Good to be True?

Cohen's results were so extraordinary that, even as the SEC suspected insider trading and set out on a years-long investigation to bring him down, giant pension funds continued to line up around the block to invest hundreds of millions of dollars with him. Ultimately, SAC Capital paid $1.8 billion in fines, and Cohen was found to have failed to supervise his people closely enough to prevent offenses, although he was not charged with insider trading. He still invests his own capital at his successor firm, Point72 Asset Management.

Another brilliant investor over the past thirty years is Israel "Izzy" Englander, founder and chairman of Millennium Management, which he started with $35 million in 1989 and now has $36 *billion* in total assets under management. That is a thousandfold increase. He has racked up average annual returns of 10 percent over the life of his fund, with a standard deviation of only three.

This means his fund had a very narrow range of actual and possible outcomes, even taken out to 95 percent certainty (and two standards of deviation), falling within the range of 16 percent at the best and *still*-up 4 percent at the worst. Underlying math: Avg. Annual Return of 10% + 3 + 3 = 16% maximum upside.

Avg. Annual Return of 10% – 3 – 3 = 4% maximum downside.

A 10 percent average annual return and a standard deviation of only three: the performance is so stellar that Bernie Madoff claimed similar numbers for the funds he ran—and he was convicted of staging one of the largest Ponzi schemes of all time. (He stole $8 billion in investors' funds and told them it had turned into $65 billion, which it had not).

The broad US stock market trades shares of more than 3,500 publicly held companies with average annual returns of 7.48 percent and a standard deviation of sixteen. It means in a year you could lose 24 percent—which is way too high! This is why no one should invest all of their assets in stocks; you lower the standard deviation of your account over all by adding varied assets with narrower ranges of possible investment outcomes.

Biotechnology stocks tend to be very volatile. That's because the price of a stock will depend on how the company's latest drug trials perform and whether the results (and the ensuing media coverage) are good or bad. Snack food stocks tend to be more stable because snack foods have pretty consistent demand, so the earnings tend to be predictable.

In addition to looking at the standard deviation of a particular stock and its historical ups and downs, an investor can look at one stock's deviation from the market overall. Walmart, for example, has a very low correlation to the stock market, a standard deviation of 0.18, which means the stock matches the market only 18 percent of the time.

All of this predictive odds-making is based on spinning out possible outcomes based on results seen over the prior decade or more. Ignore the Wall Street maxim that says past returns offer no guarantee of future results. Indeed, they do fall short of a 100 percent guarantee, yet past returns *can* provide a good picture of the range of outcomes your portfolio might encounter in the next year.

Whatever steps you take to reduce your portfolio's standard deviation, thereby reducing risk and volatility in your account, you must ensure that your returns still can keep up with your personal inflation rate—the rise in your cost of living. Inflation is eating away at your fortune to a deeper degree than the federal government wants to admit. As a result, millions of Americans are falling further behind, even as they believe they are holding their own. The seriousness of this situation, in the big picture, occurred to me as the result of a particularly personal object lesson from my mother. In the next chapter I will teach you what she taught me.

# CHAPTER 5

# Understating COLA

Wh, while my father was larger-than-life and one of the hardest-working people I have ever known, my mother may have been fiercer still, the real keystone of our family.

Lois Tublin was born and raised in Baltimore. At twenty-one she met my dad on the Boardwalk in Atlantic City, New Jersey, and a few years later they married. She had four children in seven years (I came along third, after a son and a daughter, before a second daughter). My mother spent her years making life better for the rest of us, and one of her greatest assets was her unrelenting optimism.

When we were frightened as kids because of thunder and lightning, my mother would say, "I see the sun about to come out." I carry on with her ability to look on the bright side. When I step up to the tee to start a round of golf, I know sand traps and lakes and other hazards are lurking on the course, but I ignore them, refuse to look at them. Recognizing them and talking about them is a sure bet I will end up in them.

My mother also taught me one of the most important lessons in investing, one that everybody should know, one that would underscore just how bad a job Wall Street does in managing people's money. I am talking about inflation.

I prefer to think of it as Cost of Living Adjustment, or COLA, and you will see why in a moment. By COLA, my meaning is the *increase* in the cost of living that infects and affects our daily lives.

Of the eight kinds of risk we mapped out in Chapter Three, inflation risk may be the most devious, dangerous, and difficult to diagnose. Given enough time, it can erode the real value of a retirement fund even more than stock-market losses. Yet the most respected names on Wall Street, Morgan Stanley among them, do little to train their sales forces to be on the lookout for inflation as part of their strategy for portfolio construction or to offer ways to help offset its deleterious effects on client wealth.

Most people know inflation as a matter of how much prices are rising as tracked by the Consumer Price Index (CPI), issued by the federal Bureau of Labor Statistics. The CPI uses a theoretical basket of products, goods, and services—some 80,000 different things—to tote up how much they currently cost compared with how much they cost last month and last year.

If you believe the CPI, inflation in the US has been running at 2 percent annually since 2008. Are you seeing that in *your* life? Doubtful. My guess is 7 percent a year would be more accurate for many of us; in Dallas, where I live and work, the cost of living is rising at 9 percent a year.

Given this gap between the CPI and the real rise in your cost of living, you should assume that your personal inflation rate is double or triple the CPI and ensure, if possible, that your portfolio can grow at that higher rate or better. Most Wall Street houses fail to take into account actual price increases in the client's own life. This is why my CHIP Score method is so critical to smart investing: it may be the only financial-evaluation regimen in the world to take into account an investor's personal COLA when figuring out whether his portfolio can earn enough to let him stay at par in purchasing power.

The CPI forms the basis for a trillion dollars a year in government benefits paid to more than sixty million Social Security recipients, and when the CPI goes up, the government bumps up their payments commensurately. Thus, the government and other parties have an interest in understating the real rate of inflation to hold down future benefit payments. We will tackle that topic in the next chapter.

My keener awareness of the risks of inflation came to me belatedly, seven years into my career as an adviser, when I visited my mother for one of the last times before she passed away. It was February 1994 and my mother had divorced my father and was living on her own in Chappaqua, fighting lung cancer, and unaware she had only a few months left to live. The cancer had spread to her brain though she did not yet know it.

I had been flying from Dallas to New York most weekends to see her as she endured chemotherapy and its devastating effects. On February 12, my thirty-second birthday, I wanted to spend it with my mother, as it might be the last one we would celebrate. At the airport in Dallas, I learned the Northeast was gripped in an epic snowstorm, the biggest in fifteen years.

I told the gate agent I was trying to spend my birthday with my ill mother and asked him to get me any flight in that direction. Please. He got me to Chicago, where I searched for a connecting flight to New York and repeated my story to an American Airlines agent, who told me, "There's not a chance in the world anything's going to open up."

Two hours later, out of nowhere, I heard my name over the PA speakers; I showed up at the gate and an agent, in a last-second rush, skipped any ticketing and told me, "Just get on the plane."

It was a flight to Harrisburg, Pennsylvania, another step closer. When we landed I grabbed my carry-on Morgan Stanley & Co. bag and started hitchhiking. The snowstorm was still blowing hard, the roads were icy and slick, but finally a trucker picked me up. I just came right out with it: It's my birthday, I'm trying to get to my mom to celebrate it with her because it may be our last one, she has lung cancer. She's in Chappaqua.

Now on a mission of mercy, the trucker got on his CB radio and recruited other truckers to join him in an amazing feat of kindness. They set up a kind of relay race, with me as their baton. The first trucker drove with me for several hours before handing me off to the next one, who kindly took me with him on his route as far as he could and then dropped me off for the next driver, who already was there and waiting for my arrival. This went on for what may have been a total of seven trucks—seven kind strangers, men who had no reason to help me other than the goodness and generosity in their hearts.

It was late afternoon by the time I showed up on Mom's doorstep. The last time I had seen her, she was especially frail. The chemo had made her lose most of her hair, which I had expected but it also seemed to have drained some of her obstinate spirit, consumed some vibrant part of her. This had surprised and shocked me. I worried what I might find this time.

I knocked. No answer. The front door always was unlocked so I went in. She had bought the condo after the divorce, when I was still in college. "Half a house," she called it. I looked around but she was nowhere to be seen. This worried me. The snowfall had made the roads especially dicey, and my mom should not be out and about, driving around in this mess.

This was well before cell phones remember, so I borrowed a car and started driving around looking for her, visiting neighbors and the hospital. She had developed an obsession with crusty, toasted Thomas English muffins so I stopped in grocery stores too; maybe she was out for an emergency pickup.

## "Where the Hell Have You Been?"

I returned to her home, unsuccessful, and sat down to wait, hoping she was okay. Finally around seven p.m., Mom walked in, barely surprised to see me.

"Where the hell have you *been*?" I asked her.

Mom: "Your *fucking father* didn't adjust my alimony for COLA!" I blurted out, "Mom, you drink Tab," and she said, "No, my Cost of Living Adjustment." Now puzzled, I asked, "What is that?" and she shamed me: "Edward, you don't know what a COLA is? How could you not know that?"

Clearly despite the chemo she still had plenty of grit and backbone left, and, man oh man, my mom was so right—how could I have been so clueless on COLA? Working on Wall Street for seven years by this time, I should have been fluent in inflation and COLAs and the whole bit, and yet I had no idea what a COLA was, and it wasn't front and center for anyone else in the business, either. That gnawed at me.

My mother was losing purchasing power and feeling the effects of it every day. So much so that recently she had taken a new job to bring in more income, working in sales at Saks Fifth Avenue in White Plains, N.Y., without telling any of her family.

Even more stubbornly, she had insisted on heading out into the blinding snowstorm to make it to work that day, even though twenty-one inches of snow would fall on the area. That night she was returning home from a full day at the Saks counter. Think about that: my mother, after being a homemaker for thirty years, had taken a job to fight the effects of inflation, even though she was fifty-seven years old and wore a wig to hide the effects of chemo. She still went out there every day and took care of things on her own. True grit. I wish she would have asked me for a little help, but that just wasn't her way.

When clients are behind in retirement savings and ask me what they can do to catch up, some will balk when I advise taking a second or even a third job. My own mother got a job while battling cancer. Don't tell me it can't be done.

My mother passed two months later. It hit me hard and still hurts. Soon after, it occurred to me that, while she had died before inflation could lay waste to an even bigger chunk of her life savings, what about millions of retirees who live far longer? What will happen to their accounts? Devastation may be the answer for many of them, even those with blue-chip-branded wealth advisers.

From that moment forward, whenever I thought about how clueless Wall Street was on COLA and risk, I would recall the frightened look on my mom's face as she asked me to reassure her: "Am I okay? Is this going to be all right?" Nobody should have feel that insecure and vulnerable. I vowed to find a better answer, and as I began to develop the CHIP Score, she was always at the forefront of my mind. There were many other Loises in the world, just as frightened as my mother, not knowing what they should do and being led astray by an industry that pretended it could help them.

In the ensuing years, I researched inflation and pored over academic studies and articles on the real increase in the cost of living. The research of the late pollster Albert Sindlinger, who claimed to have coined the term consumer confidence, surprised and alarmed me. He had asked consumers the same four questions about their economic outlook every year since 1955, compiling a Household Money Supply Index that measured household liquidity.

A *New York Times* profile of Sindlinger, published a year before my mother's death, said, "One striking result [of his polling] is that consumers almost invariably find inflation higher than is shown by the Bureau of Labor Statistics. His own cost-of-living index now shows an annual rate of increase of about 8.25 percent after being between 9 and 10 percent much of the year. These rates are three to five times the increases shown by the Labor Department's Consumer Price Index."

My research also led me to economist Walter J. "John" Williams and his website on CPI chicanery and inflation, ShadowStats.com. He has said the intentional skewing of CPI has deprived Social Security recipients of fully half of what they otherwise would be receiving if their COLA increases matched the real rise in prices that has been going on for twenty or thirty years.

A couple of years after I left Morgan Stanley, I opened my own firm, Chapwood Investments. A few months in, I reached out to Williams to ask about his research, and we struck up a correspondence. We have chatted a few dozen times in the ensuing years, mostly by phone. Early on, I brought up the need for separate COLA indexes, depending on location. Costs in New York City rise 10 percent a year but go up only 3 percent in Taos, New Mexico. The biggest reason for that difference is taxes—*tax-flation*, as I called it.

Higher taxes in New York create higher prices for everything, and the bite they take out of people's pockets adds up over the years. So do the lost opportunities, in terms of what other necessities that money might have purchased if it hadn't been collected in taxes. Yet the government's CPI doesn't take into account the differences in state and local tax rates in various places and their impact on spending behavior; just as it gives short shrift to another big factor in your personal cost of living, the high costs of health care.

Toward this end, I lobbied Williams to do a thorough city-by-city survey of real prices. "Mr. Williams," I told him, "you need to do COLA per city. You are missing a really important element—tax-flation. Taxes are the number one reason costs go up for consumers."

"Eddie, you are absolutely right, but I don't have time to do it," he responded. It was just too much extra hassle, he told me, and I thought, "Well, I guess I'll do it."

My plan was to gather the shifting prices for 500 of the most frequently purchased products in the top fifty markets in the country. After I assembled the list of cities, I checked it against my friend list on Facebook and found I had a pal in every market except two: Wichita, Kansas, and Taos, New Mexico. I reached out to the bunch of them, telling them of my interest in tracking prices.

Most referred me to someone who would be more interested in taking part in my experiment. Our price index made its debut a few months later, and we named it the Chapwood Index. It included not only product prices, but also local average costs for personal taxes, health insurance, mortgage payments, and so on. Our index showed that, in many markets, prices were increasing much faster than the CPI measured.

In my hometown of Dallas, the Chapwood Index had prices rising 9.4 percent. In a lot of cities, the price of popcorn at the movie theater was spiking hard. The cost of a bagel was going up fifteen cents in many places—that translates to an extra fifty-five dollars a year for a bagel a day. We still update the Chapwood Index every six months to get a more realistic view of the true price movements in people's lives.

Research elsewhere also underscored the corrosive effects of falling behind in purchasing power. US bonds kept up with the rise in inflation only 17 percent of the time from 1997 through 2011, one article reported. If you earned 2 percent a year on a ten-year Treasury note until maturity, your return after taxes was only 1.3 percent (at a 35 percent federal rate). Yet inflation averaged almost 3 percent in that same fifteen-year span, so you were down 25 percent or more in purchasing power by the end of that period.

By contrast, stock prices can rise with inflation because companies often possess pricing power in an inflationary cycle, boosting their reported earnings. From 1926 to 2011, the S&P 500 returned almost 10 percent a year, seven points better than the inflation rate for consumer prices in that same period, according to data from the financial research firm Ibbotson Associates.

## A 'Larcenous Villain'

Money manager David Dreman of the Value Index Fund has called inflation a "larcenous villain." He pointed out in early 2015 that thirty-year Treasury bonds yielded 2.82 percent and would net only 0.75 percent annually after accounting for 2 percent inflation and taxes. "If inflation increases to 4% it will have a disastrous effect on safe-money savers," he writes. "Indeed, this strategy wiped out a good part of the financially conservative wealthy after World War II, as the dollar lost 92% of its purchasing power from 1945 to the present time." How devastating. I read that and felt absolutely shocked.

Though few people on Wall Street seem to pay attention to inflation and its pernicious effects, you can reconstruct your portfolio to anticipate and offset it by using my CHIP Score system. All you need do is to read the rest of this book; but first, young Jedi, you must understand more about the invisible and visible forces of inflation and COLA.

Inflation is everywhere and all around us, like the Force in *Star Wars*. Monthly rents are up overall by more than 70 percent from 2000 to 2018. That is up an average of more than 3 percent a year, which is almost 50 percent higher than the rate of inflation reflected in the CPI overall, which rose only 2.09 percent annually in the same period.

Cell phones, streaming services, and internet access have added hundreds of dollars a month to each person's tab, expenses that didn't exist twenty years ago.

The starting price of a weekend family package at Disney World has doubled in ten years, now up to almost $2,800. Movie theaters now charge an average of almost ten bucks a head, up 30 percent in a decade; in New York the ticket price can be as high as seventeen dollars. The average monthly cable bill now is at a hundred dollars, and for years it has been rising at three or four times the rate of inflation. Pay-per-view movies at home cost the cable company pennies to deliver but cost viewers six dollars a pop, and though tech costs fall 15 percent to 30 percent a year overall, the movie price holds firm or rises.

To be sure, the CPI may overstate, rather than understate, some elements of inflation by failing to account for falling costs elsewhere. Advances in technology and declining costs per unit of computing power can be difficult to trace and assess. Example: Storage costs fall 30 percent to 40 percent per year, encouraging some big companies to make ever larger purchases, so much so that they end up spending more than they were spending before. Should that count as deflationary or inflationary?

Though the media lament slack wage increases and declining purchasing power for American consumers, they fail to talk about how many items are far cheaper than they were twenty or thirty years ago, in terms of how many days of work at average wages it takes to pay for a particular appliance at current prices.

Some examples, from a recent article that culled prices from the old Sears catalog in 1975 and compared them with prices nowadays: In 1975, when worker wages averaged $4.87 per hour, you had to work sixty hours to buy a nineteen-inch color TV set; in 2013, when worker wages neared twenty dollars per hour, a similar TV set required less than seven hours of work. We went from seven-and-a-half days of labor to less than one day.

Buying a refrigerator took almost sixty-eight hours of work in 1975, compared with twenty hours in 2013; a washer-dryer required sixty-eight hours of labor back then, and it took only thirty hours of work in 2013. Or, looked at another way, in 1970 the cost of a washing machine was equal to 8 percent of average annual earnings, and by 2011 the cost was just 1.5 percent of average annual wages.

These changes in prices result from efficiencies of mass production, cheaper manufacturing offshore, leaner back-office operations and better-targeted marketing. It is questionable how good a job the CPI does at ingesting those and other variables as it spins out the official version of what is happening to prices in the economy. This is true, no matter how great the minds at the Bureau of Labor Statistics.

Rising prices, however, are only a *symptom* of inflation. Technically speaking, inflation is an increase in the supply of money available to chase after goods; it is better known for the increasing prices that are a byproduct of inflation.

Say you do business in an especially small, sealed-off economy where only a million one-dollar bills are in circulation for all commerce, and everything is priced accordingly. Now let's say you suddenly print another million one-dollar bills and put them into circulation; this inflation of the money supply will let more people seek a raise or impose higher prices.

By doubling the supply of one-dollar bills in your teensy economy, however, you also reduce the value of each dollar by half, because when the supply of anything soars, the value per unit goes down accordingly. The Law of Supply and Demand writ small.

The real problem emerges when everyone inside this sealed micro-economy begins to expect prices to rise, because this expectation changes their behavior—they start buying bigger supplies of a given thing now to avoid paying more later. This psychological shift fuels even higher prices, creating a destructive, self-sustaining cycle.

Now, let's zoom out to the massive $19 trillion-a-year US economy, still the world's largest by far (China is number two at $11 trillion). This cycle, in part, is how we got to double-digit inflation during the back half of the '70s and the administration of President Jimmy Carter. To tame this roaring, destructive dragon, the US central bank, the Federal Reserve, raised interest rates to a suffocating high of 14.8 percent in 1980.

At the time, the misery index, developed by economist Arthur Okun, became a household phrase that helped Ronald Reagan wrest the presidency from Carter in 1980. The misery index is equal to the inflation rate plus the unemployment rate, and during the Carter presidency it hit a high of 19.9. under President Reagan, the index hit a low of 7.7 by December 1986. The December 2018 misery index was even lower, at 5.8.

The misery index: imagine what it is like to have created something that has significant meaning and utility for the financial world. To be a wee bit grandiose about it, my dream is that the CHIP Score catches on that way, helping millions of people avoid financial anorexia by giving them a clear grading system for vetting their advisers and forcing them to improve their services.

The Fed plays a central role in the economy—even more so now, after the market meltdown and the shock-and-awe government bailout of nineteen Wall Street banks a decade ago. The Fed sets key, base interest rates on major banks' overnight lending to one another as the foundation for all other interest rates, and it controls how much credit is created for the banking system.

Thus the Fed is said to control the money supply, although the Treasury Department controls the printing presses and designates how much currency is in circulation. The Federal Reserve tightens and loosens its grip on these two chokepoints (interest rates, money supply) as it serves its mandate, consisting of three goals:

- attaining and sustaining full employment, or as close to it as possible;
- keeping prices stable, restraining inflation to a target of 2 percent per year;
- maintaining moderate long-term interest rates.

**Game of Expectations**

The most important of these three goals may be stable prices—and the *expectation* of stable prices on the part of consumers and the markets. A sudden outbreak of inflation can spread quickly through the economy, surprising businesses and investors and undermining the other two goals (full employment and moderate interest rates).

To Fed officials, it's all a head game. To them, the most important factor is how consumers are *feeling* about inflation—never mind what's happening to prices or the spending patterns of people right now, the pivot point is what might they do *next*? Are their expectations changing—becoming unmoored, in Fed-speak—for where prices are headed? If they begin to anticipate higher prices, prices *will rise* and inflation *will* get worse, in part simply because we expected that to happen.

Like standing at the golf tee and focusing too much on the sand trap.

Thus, the Fed endeavors to preempt mere *expectations* of rising prices, an even more elusive goal than restraining prices themselves. Wall Street, for its part, watches the Fed's every move, hiccup, statement, answer, and sideways glance and parses it for some new clue that inflation expectations are becoming unmoored, and thus the Fed may raise interest rates, crimping economic growth and hurting stock prices and who knows what else.

One of the biggest fears now dogging investors—the bearish and circumspect among them, at any rate—is that rampant, uncontrollable inflation could break out again. The rather stunning fact is that this has yet to happen, when by some measures it should have happened.

In the Great Meltdown of 2008, the once-roaring US housing market suddenly tumbled, a global recession took hold, a credit squeeze strangled lending and sparked a rise in defaults, and the Federal Reserve and government officials had to intervene aggressively to stem a worldwide panic. The Fed mounted an intentional, strategic, massive increase in US currency and capital to prop up the economy.

As the Federal Reserve moved boldly to stave off global economic collapse and a second Great Depression, it took extraordinary actions on two urgent fronts: it slashed base interest rates to almost zero to encourage easier credit and lending, and it imposed a massive increase in the supply of freshly created dollars in the economy.

To help keep interest rates low and boost the tepid rebound, the Fed spent more than $3 trillion—money it never really had—to buy US Treasury bonds, real estate bonds whose prices had collapsed, and other securities. This policy was called Quantitative Easing (QE), a soothing phrase that sounds like a format for Lite FM radio. Overall, the QE program swelled the Fed's balance sheet of assets it owns from less than $1 trillion to $4.5 trillion—thereby quadrupling its balance sheet in a few years. The enormity of it is almost unfathomable. You are talking a surge of newly created money or credit equivalent to roughly 25 percent of US Gross Domestic Product (GDP).

The Fed program was like one massive government-bond Ponzi scheme. In essence, the Treasury printed up new bonds as a promise to pay: hand us millions of dollars now and we will pay you interest on it for a bond duration of anywhere from one month to thirty years and pay you back the full original sum at the end of the bond's term. Treasury sold these bonds to Wall Street firms, which re-sold them to the Federal Reserve and pocketed a tidy little profit of "golden crumbs" (from *Bonfire of the Vanities*, may Tom Wolfe rest in peace). The Fed legally is prohibited from buying government bonds directly from the Treasury department, so Wall Street acts as the middleman and skims a "vig," the vigorish, just as mob bookies do on illegal sports betting.

Since the Fed quadrupled the total size of the balance sheet, prices in the US generally should have risen faster in response, at least somewhere, to absorb the surge in the supply of new dollars and capital coursing through the economy. Recall my example of the sealed, one-million-dollar micro-economy that suddenly has two million one-dollar bills in circulation: the currency should be worth less—have less purchasing power—than when half as many copies of it were available.

The surprise is that inflation, according to government numbers, has remained a mild pussycat rather than turn into a roaring dragon. In rebounding from the meltdown a decade ago, prices were restrained in part by the fact that the severe downturn had whacked business activity so hard that it slowed the velocity of money, how many times it was changing hands in the economy.

Slow velocity of money, however, cannot explain why inflation has stayed dormant all these years. A much bigger factor is at work in this surprising absence of an inflation breakout, and that is the design of the Consumer Price Index, which lowballs the real rise in prices. This is costing Americans billions of dollars in lost purchasing power and unpaid benefit increases, and the biggest sham and scandal of it all is that this is by design, by tacit government conspiracy, and just about everybody is in on it—Wall Street included.

The whole world is out of whack, and one of the key metrics we use to track it, CPI, is even more out of whack. How wacky is that? You will see what I mean, up next.

# CHAPTER 6

# CPI and the Big Lie

Newsflash, this just in: The CPI is a Great Big Lie.

I am talking about the Consumer Price Index, the running guesstimate by which the government tracks whether prices are going up or down in our economy, and by how much and in what sectors, and for which products and services, all with an eye toward divining what that might mean for economic growth and consumer behavior. As gauged officially by the CPI, the inflation boogeyman has been cast in the title role of *Waiting for Godot*—it never seems to arrive.

There may be only one plausible explanation for why the CPI says inflation is tamed and has been limping along for years. For many years the Consumer Price Index has been chronically low-balling true inflation and underestimating the real price increases that affect consumers' daily lives. Worse, the CPI's low-balling tacitly is intentional, a de facto conspiracy by the US government, Wall Street, and corporate pension plans to restrain increases in benefits paid to retirees across America.

When inflation rises, as tracked by the government's CPI, the recipients get a bump up to match it. It is called a COLA, Cost of Living

Adjustment (as my mother had to explain to me on that visit home in 1994, much to my chagrin). Take a more conservative approach that holds down the real rise in prices, and you tamp down the rising costs of Social Security and pension plans. Hold down the COLA and the savings can stack up over the ensuing decades, compounding into hundreds and hundreds of billions of dollars in benefits that the government won't have to pay out.

This is pretty much what the government did in the '80s and '90s by fiddling with the components of the Consumer Price Index. This Big Lie may help the government's balance sheet, and it may extend the financial viability of Social Security for extra years, yet it means millions of older Americans are falling farther behind to the real *increase* in the cost of living every year.

Social Security payments now total $1 trillion a year paid to sixty-three million Americans; this includes $720 billion for forty-seven million retirees age sixty-five and older, and another ten thousand Americans turn age sixty-five every day—for the next nineteen years. (Technically, the age at which Social Security pays full benefits is sixty-six years and two months.) In January 2018, the COLA was a 2 percent raise in monthly benefits, as if the cost of living for Social Security recipients rose only 2 percent in the previous year. That, of course, is bunkum. Try closer to 7 percent and you are closer to the truth for many Americans.

It is the *increase* in the cost of the life you live that should be your main concern. Whatever your cost of living might be, it is what it is—the bigger question is, what is the real rise in that base cost and are your investments and earnings growing enough to cover that increase?

Most wealth managers are failing to take this into account for their clients, and this makes my portfolio-evaluation method, the CHIP Score, all the more important to safeguarding your investments. It may be the only portfolio-vetting regimen to take into account the individual investor's personal inflation rate, his COLA, and the rate of return needed to stay on pace with the rising prices in his life.

If costs are going up 7 percent a year in your life even as the CPI says the rise is 2 percent, pretty soon your purchasing power has plunged by one-third. This spells disaster for retirees and the economy. Worse, many people are unaware of this erosion because they believe another government lie—that it will pay them a fair COLA to ensure their pension and Social Security payments keep up with the rise in their cost of living.

This is so sad, and the effects show up gradually. Your parents stop taking vacations to Europe, the birthday gifts they hand out to your kids get skimpier, a new look of worry haunts them. These people have no idea of the fraud that the government has perpetrated upon them. Wealth advisers and Wall Street are complicit in this looming crisis, owing to their ignorance about inflation and how to deal with it properly.

We must find a better way to invest if we are to protect ourselves. That is the purpose of my CHIP Score, and teaching you how to use it is the purpose of this book.

* * *

Your investment adviser likely is insufficiently concerned about the COLA in your life and how to offset it in your portfolio. Your personal cost-of-living increase is likely to be running at two to three times the inflation rate claimed by the government, as reported in the Consumer Price Index. You must plan accordingly and ensure your investments can earn enough to offset the rising prices in your life.

In tracking inflation and where prices are headed (up or down and how fast they are going in either direction), the Consumer Price Index is based on a theoretical "basket" filled with not just food but also prod-ucts, services, fuel, and other basic costs of living, inputs numbering in the thousands. This is an enormously complicated and intricate under-taking, especially for a decades-old index struggling to keep up with radical changes in consumer shopping since the rise of Amazon and the steady demise of the American shopping mall.

CPI's fundamental flaw, though, is that it seems secretly skewed and designed by intent to keep everything down to a dull roar. Most of the media coverage of the index seems rigged, too. Government economists exclude the volatile costs of food and energy and talk about "core" (read: lower) inflation, yet how many people can manage to exclude the costs of eating and driving from their lives?

Statisticians smooth out the numbers and adjust for seasonal variations and changes in the year-ago numbers, yet if your monthly rent just jumped up 15 percent from last month to this month, you feel the impact instantly. No smoothing out is available for you.

## A Dormant Dragon

Still, we know that government tells all of us that inflation is tame, the dragon is dormant, and yet many of us know inherently that the CPI is understating the price increases we see in our daily lives. It is kind of like when you were seven years old and you learned, for the first time, that the whole Santa Claus thing was one Big Lie—and everybody was in on it.

The CPI came into use as a government indicator for the economy after World War II, and unions began tying wage increases in their contracts to CPI. In 1935, Congress passed the Social Security Act, beginning government payments to retired workers in 1940. Workers started paying a payroll tax into a government trust, the Social Security Fund, content in knowing the money would be invested conservatively and the benefits would be paid out to them upon retirement.

From 1940 to 1975, Congress boosted the monthly benefits that retirees received to offset inflation, generously granting eleven such increases in those thirty-five years, with the average increase around 5.7 percent per year. Thus it was an annual raise of almost 6 percent, every year, for millions of recipients to keep up with inflation.

In 1975, the Social Security payments began to be pegged to the increase in the Consumer Price Index, moving up in lockstep with the

CPI each year. Now Congress wouldn't have to pass laws every few years to authorize an increase in benefit payments. It would be automatic.

Makes sense, no? The government wanted to be fair to everyone. Inflation is a natural part of the economy, and it was in everyone's best interest that people get a little bump to their Social Security check to keep up. Automatic raises—this is one way deficits grow, decades later, on the good intentions of politicians seeking automatic reelection.

In the '70s, the Social Security budget was small compared with that of today, so tossing in almost a 6 percent raise every year was no big deal. By 1980, however, the US inflation rate hit a staggering 14.8 percent as measured by the CPI. In some ways it was a warning sign that this could end up getting exorbitantly expensive.

So, in the '80s, ever so subtly, the Bureau of Labor Statistics began tinkering with the formula for the CPI, which had the effect of lowering the reported rise in prices overall. The bureau switched from mathematical weighting to geometric weighting, automatically reducing the weight of goods that are rising in price. Furthermore, the bureau began "re-weighting" components of the basket every two years instead of every ten, adding to wiggle room for adjustments and manipulation.

By the '90s, the tinkering continued as inflation simmered at 3 percent or so, and the government had a rare bout of fiscal frugality (albeit a short-lived one). The Republican-controlled Congress suddenly focused with rat-like cunning on the deficit and how to cut it. It had begun dawning on Washington that the COLA was a ticking time bomb for entitlements. What if inflation and the CPI rocketed back up to 14 percent again one day?

Payments to retirees would have to go up commensurately. These higher entitlement payments, every year compounded on top of the last one, would strain the already teetering finances of the Social Security program. The explosion in benefit payments would require big increases in payroll taxes or big reductions in monthly Social Security checks, and either path could get incumbents voted out of office.

Thus, the feds and the big spenders in both political parties had reason to root for a CPI that claims inflation is as tame as it can get. How to make this happen?

In the end, Washington politicians and bureaucrats cheated. In the mid-1990s they changed how the CPI was calculated, so that the reported increase in the prices of goods and services was lower than what was really happening in the economy—and in Americans' lives. This disparity between real price increases and CPI's lesser increases is so bad that our CHIP Score portfolio rating system dispenses with the CPI numbers altogether; instead, it uses an assumption that your personal inflation rate is double or triple the rise in the CPI, and your target for returns must be set accordingly.

In fiddling with CPI, government officials did so under the guise of aiming to make the CPI *better* at measuring inflation. Two feet good, four feet *better*. At the time, some experts maintained the CPI was *overstating* inflation, and that fixing it to be more accurate could offer the benefit of "bending the cost curve" of Social Security benefit payments and other government entitlement programs. Curb benefit increases and you could make the programs more financially stable.

In January 1995, Federal Reserve Chairman Alan Greenspan testified to Congress and said the CPI was overstating the real rises in prices in the US economy. This generated a lot of talk, and soon afterward House Speaker Newt Gingrich was in the *New York Times* openly discussing how fixing CPI could have implications for lower spending on Social Security and provide "maneuvering room" for budget negotiations.

Later on he reportedly told a Clinton administration official at the Bureau of Labor Statistics, "If you could see your way clear to doing these things, we might have more money for BLS programs."

Congress commissioned a blue-ribbon panel to study the matter and named Michael Boskin to head it; he had been chairman of the Council of Economic Advisers for President George H.W. Bush. In late

1996, the Boskin Commission report on the CPI came out. It argued that the CPI had been *overstating* inflation by 1.3 percentage points for decades and recommended a rather startling downward adjustment of 1.1 percentage points in the reported CPI for 1996 of 3.3 percent.

The Boskin report singled out a key flaw in the CPI: it lacked an ability to reflect "the substitution effect." This is the notion that a person who eats steak will trade down to hamburger (or chicken, as the Boskin report cited) when the price of steak rises too high; thus, the switch to a cheaper protein should count as being deflationary because it cuts the inflationary effects of a price rise for steak.

To me, this is flawed logic. If the consumer must trade down and no longer can buy his favorite ribeye, he is settling for a lower standard of living to offset the effects of his rising costs. How can this be a good thing that holds *down* the inflation rate? It fails to reflect the retreat of our giving up things we used to enjoy because we have lost too much purchasing power.

One purpose of the CHIP Score is to give you an instant reading on whether your financial adviser has designed your portfolio with COLA in mind, aiming for returns that can offset prices that are rising a lot faster than the CPI will admit.

## The Fix Is In

Up until this time, the CPI had been based on a fixed basket of the same goods and services tracked monthly, comparing their price changes without regard to whether consumers had shifted their purchases to a cheaper item. This fixed-basket approach has been the preferred method of producing a pricing index since the eighteenth century.

Using a fixed basket, the CPI measured what was happening to the cost of maintaining the same standard of living; revising the CPI to be more of a substitution-based index reduced the reported rise in prices and became more of a subsistence index.

As my economist pal John Williams put it in an article in 2004: "Cost of living was being replaced by the cost of survival. The old system told you how much you had to increase your income in order to keep buying steak. The new system promised you hamburger, and then dog food, perhaps, after that..."

An ensuing backlash killed any chance that Congress would act officially on the CPI, but the BLS quietly began fiddling with the system to the same effect, shifting from a fixed basket of goods to a morphing basket based on more of a substitution-oriented outlook.

"The plan was to reduce cost of living adjustments for government payments to Social Security recipients, etc. The cuts in reported inflation were an effort to reduce the federal deficit without anyone in Congress having to do the politically impossible," Williams continued.

The CPI underwent various revisions so that today, even if prices really were rising 10 percent or more annually, the increase would appear as if it were only 3.5 percent or so. Williams has argued that the CPI understates real inflation by seven percentage points because of "redefinitions" and "flawed methodologies."

These changes, together with earlier adjustments in the Carter and Reagan administrations, "have reduced current Social Security payments by roughly half from where they would have been otherwise. That means Social Security checks today would be about double had the various changes not been made," Williams wrote.

This absolutely stuns me. Our own federal officials and politicians conspired to cheat retired Americans out of the COLA increases that might have let them avoid making sacrifices in their lifestyle (such as trading down to hamburger from filet mignon). My mother struggled with rising prices in the closing months of her life, and other aging women are in danger of outliving their money and losing ground to inflation every year. I created the CHIP Score to help them avert this unfortunate financial fate.

The Big Lie of the CPI creates a massive reality-distortion field. In addition to invisibly reducing the rise in COLA for Social Security payments, this ineffective CPI recalculation also restrained increases in pension plans for government workers and private sector retirees, and in wages and benefits for union contracts, especially for government workers. Wages have gone almost nowhere in inflation-adjusted terms, and one thing constraining wages is the widespread and misinformed belief that inflation in the economy is moribund.

Also, the lower-skewed CPI reassures and soothes the markets and the masses. The public's forward-looking expectations then can continue to be that inflation will remain low, because that is what the numbers are telling us—and remember, expectations are everything to the Fed.

The positive-feedback loop continues: consumers' unchanged consumption patterns and stable expectations let the Fed stop worrying about inflation and forgo raising interest rates too much, which otherwise could hamper business expansion; this cheers the markets, and a month later comes the next CPI report, and the cycle renews.

CPI's understating price increases offers still another upside for policymakers: it lowers the GDP deflator, the measure that government economists use to calculate *real* GDP growth after discounting inflation. Thus, GDP growth looks stronger than it really is.

This unreality also boosts stock prices. If inflation is low, then the interest rates paid for borrowing can be lower, too, and the acceptable price-to-earnings ratio (P/E) for stocks can be higher than it would have been otherwise. (Price-to-earnings ratio is a way of valuing and comparing all stocks; to buy a share of Amazon that will earn all of, say seven dollars in a year, you have to pay roughly $1,800, for a price-to-earnings multiple of 257. The average P/E is around eighteen.)

As a rule, when the interest rate on borrowing is 5 percent, the equivalent P/E ratio for stocks is twenty; when borrowing costs only 2.5

percent, the buyer can pay more, and a stock's P/E could be forty and still seem reasonable.

To illustrate: you borrow $1 million at 5 percent interest annually to buy a business that earns $50,000 in net profit per year, just enough to cover your interest payments. If you could borrow at 2.5 percent to buy that same business, you now could pay up to $2 million for it, and still cover your interest payments of $50,000 per year.

Also, low inflation as stated in the CPI lets bond issuers pay lower interest rates overall. Rising interest rates cause the P/E ratio on stocks to go lower, in part because stock values must compete with the now-higher bond rates.

In perpetuating this Big Lie, government officials and their economists and our elected representatives mean well. If the tamped-down CPI spawns good economic sentiment, it helps the economy generally, which helps keep up good economic sentiment, which then keeps helping the economy grow.

At some point the official number is the official number, it's what everyone believes. The CPI is the instant temperature reading that connotes sickness or health of the economy. This flawed and much-watched metric may be a fantasy, yet if everyone believes it, it is every bit as real as reality is real.

The problem for consumers is that real costs are going up maybe three times as much as the newly redesigned Consumer Price Index says they are going up, so worker wages are lagging behind, hurting consumer purchasing power for workers and retirees alike.

Lower-income and middle-income folks are working harder than ever, a lot of them have trouble covering monthly expenses, and most of them lack a savings cushion of three to six months' pay. When they reach a certain threshold of pain, they will do what they must to survive. They will take an extra job, lean on the government for a subsidy, take out a payday loan, borrow from a family member, or pursue any number of solutions.

Thus, while federal officials think they pulled a fast one by manipulating CPI and trimming benefit payments by hundreds of billions of dollars over decades, they just end up paying the same tab in other ways. More of the working poor get on food stamps because their employers aren't giving out good raises, and the Medicaid rolls grow larger than ever as the costs of health care soar.

The biggest losers in the mass delusion induced by the government's Consumer Price Index are retirees. The low-balling of the CPI by our government, all but lying to us and maintaining that prices are increasing a lot less than they really are, means millions of people are falling farther behind every year. The sluggish, barely visible growth in wages in the US over the past twenty years is another outcome.

## Taking a Double Hit

A Social Security recipient takes a double hit. First, the monthly benefit payment will be lower than it otherwise would be if the CPI did a better job of capturing the full rise in prices in the economy; second, the returns on his investment portfolio are less robust than he realizes, so that a 10 percent return really might be a 3 percent return after deducting his personal inflation rate. So when you hear in the media that workers' wages are failing to keep up with inflation, the reports are more right than even the reporters realize.

Even now, government officials are eyeing still other changes in how the CPI is put together, and these changes might further drive down the reported price increases in the economy. Currently the Bureau of Labor Statistics tracks three separate price indexes: CPI-U (the price index for urban consumers), CPI-W (for all wage earners and clerical staff), and the newest one, C-CPI-U, for Chained CPI for urban consumers.

The bureau began tracking C-CPI-U monthly in August 2002, and this is the one to watch for what the government may do next to further low-ball the rises in reported CPI. CPI-W for wage earners is the metric used for Social Security COLAs, and in recent years there has been talk of switching to Chained CPI as the main standard. The idea was resurrected when President Obama's administration proposed switching to Chained CPI but got shelved. Surprise! It turns out C-CPI-U produces an even lower inflation rate than CPI-W does.

While the CPI-W and the CPI-U come out monthly and are official instantly, Chained CPI comes out monthly and is then revised quarterly so that each reading becomes official only a year after it first came out. This has the effect of smoothing out price movements and further easing the impact of the real price increases going on in the economy.

The Bureau argues that C-CPI-U is a "closer approximation" of real inflation. It is another ruse masking a cut in the payment boosts (the Cost of Living Adjustment) that Social Security otherwise would have paid. Officials admit that C-CPI-U pegs price increases as being even smaller than the rises claimed by the other two indexes. For the twelve years through 2013, the inflation reported by Chained CPI was 2.14 percent; CPI-U was 2.33 percent. That is an 8 percent lower inflation rate, and 8 percent of $1 trillion in Social Security payments annually would amount to an extra $80 billion saved per year, compounded for decades—that is $80 billion a year in benefits that never would make it to Grandma and Grandpa. Just by the sleight of hand of moving from CPI-W to C-CPI-U.

As the economist John Williams noted a few years ago:

> *"The [C-CPI-U] looks again like it has a strong chance of being used as a new federal parasite to drain consumer liquidity. Like a vampire bat that sucks only enough blood for self-nourishment— leaving its victims alive for further abuse—the use of the [C-CPI-U] as a cost of living adjustment (COLA) measure is designed to suck real disposable income from the limited cash-flow of Social Security recipients for the benefit of politicians who do not have the guts to vote against Social Security."*

For higher-income earners, this means lost purchasing power by the day, and your financial adviser is ill-equipped to help you do much to stop it. The CHIP Score will let you rate your portfolio *and* your adviser and examine the most important elements of your account.

Even the biggest Wall Street firms have neglected to train their agents to focus on their clients' personal inflation rates, so how can they know what rate of return you need to stay out in front of the real price increases affecting your life? If they don't know that, how can they be making your life better? They aren't, they are making your life worse.

Financial advisers rarely mention the CPI or inflation unless the portfolio they put together for you has a bad year. If your account goes up only 3 percent, they will say, "Hey, everything is fine. You are in a very safe portfolio, and the CPI only went up 2 percent this year. So you didn't lose purchasing power."

That is another big lie.

# CHAPTER 7

# Portfolio Construction

Someday, if you are lucky, your investments might fare so well that you have the extra scratch to afford a second home. Feeling flush, you buy a site in a seaside town and decide to design and build from the ground up. You hire a construction contractor to design this dream home and turn the blueprints into reality. He dives in, hires a crew, and finishes in record time. It looks beautiful on the outside, although on the inside your new house seems a little wobbly, maybe, now and then.

Only later do you learn that the contractor you hired never had any training in how to design a sturdy, up-to-code house, never learned how to set up the structural ridge beam to support the roof or how to pour the concrete foundation properly. As for the electrical, plumbing, and insulation his crew installed, fuhgeddaboudit.

You can see where I'm going here: most financial advisers are woefully inept at *portfolio construction,* and even big-name Wall Street firms don't train their brokers in how to do it. The investment portfolios erected by most Wall Street wealth advisers are wobbly houses designed by well-meaning guys whose main education is in how to sell investments rather than put together a safe and sound portfolio.

At one point a few years ago, I reviewed the model portfolios of the biggest names on Wall Street—J. P. Morgan Chase, Morgan Stanley, Merrill Lynch, Goldman Sachs, UBS, Fidelity Investments—and found that all of them carried more risk than what the firms' advisers were telling their clients. This inability to quantify and evaluate risk is part of the problem with bad portfolio design.

The biggest weakness in most portfolios is the lack of a special class known as non-correlated assets, investments that zig when the rest of the market zags. These contrarian instruments rise when the mainstream markets fall and head downward when the rest of the markets head upward. They are non-correlated to the movements of the broader markets, especially stocks, and the best investment advisory firms (yes, the term is relative) should constantly be hunting for non-correlated assets.

An asset that closely tracks the stock market's ups and downs 100 percent of the time has a correlation to stocks of 1.0; an uncorrelated asset is at 0.0 because it bears no similarity at all to stocks' patterns, and a non-correlated investment moves in the opposite direction of stocks.

It is an all but irrefutable truth that 97.5 percent of portfolios are fundamentally flawed and more vulnerable to higher risk and bigger losses because they lack non-correlated assets. They comprise solely publicly traded securities, and in these highly wired times of instant global communication of information, most publicly traded securities resemble each other in their price movements. They are highly correlated to one another.

Adding alternative assets is the best way to *reduce* risk and volatility in your account, because they can hold steady, or even rise, when your major holdings are tumbling downward. Many financial advisers, however, wrongly view adding alternatives as something to avoid because it may *increase* the risk of losses. They have it completely ass-backwards.

You reduce risk by padding your portfolio with assets that have different types of risk. Recall that the stock market overall has a standard deviation of sixteen and the possibility of a 20 percent loss in any given year; by adding a non-correlated asset that has an even higher standard deviation than stocks, you can reduce risk in your overall portfolio. Simply put, portfolios cannot be safe in a world where they are reliant on all asset prices going in one direction simultaneously, whether up or down.

Two common non-correlated assets are gold and Treasury bonds (an even better choice is diamonds, though most people feel safer buying gold and T-bills). When the stock market panics and prices plunge, gold prices hold their own or head up as stock investors get spooked and sell to put their proceeds into gold. Treasury prices can surge as investors rush in to buy bonds that have almost a surefire guarantee from the US government that they will get their money back, plus interest. Other non-correlated assets include precious gems, artwork, private loans to small businesses, even an investment in a professional racehorse.

Most clients mistakenly hope everything in their portfolios will do well at the same time, but if everything is doing well, that's a problem. If all the assets are trading in the same direction, you have nothing protecting you from the downside when they all take a U-turn in unison and start falling. You want some bets that will rise in value when others go down to balance out your portfolio and reduce wild swings of volatility.

A portfolio isn't entirely about return—it is about *risk-adjusted return*: how to get the strongest returns possible while minimizing the downside risk and narrowing the range of possible predictable outcomes. This means some investments should be doing well, and others not so well, or even poorly, at all times.

Constructing a portfolio that is protected is akin to playing right field in baseball. You have to be ready for anything, though most of the time a lot of nothing will happen. You may stand out there for eight innings, slack-jawed and daydreaming, and all of a sudden a ball gets hit in your direction and the game's fate rides on your glove. You have to be in the right place at the right time to perform at your best.

## An Elusive Asset

In investing, if your portfolio lacks non-correlated assets, it cannot perform as you had hoped. The real challenge is that it is getting more and more difficult to ferret out good, non-correlated assets to fill out your portfolio and help you reduce risk. What used to work doesn't work anymore, and your broker probably has scant awareness of this. A lot of Wall Street firms still are asleep to the notion that a global convergence of correlation is at hand, and that they must broaden the search for offbeat assets.

A couple of decades ago, overseas stocks and emerging markets were non-correlated to US stocks, and you could hedge your US investments by buying stocks on exchanges in Indonesia or Vietnam. Today they all move in lockstep. International stocks in developed nations have a correlation to US stocks of 0.94, meaning they act similarly to US equities 94 percent of the time and deviate only 6 percent of the time; previously they deviated from US moves half the time.

Non-correlated assets were everywhere decades ago, in a slower-moving world that lacked speed-of-light fiber optics, the internet, 24/7 news networks, day trading, smartphones, and other modern mainstays. The more connected everyone gets, the more ubiquitous and fast-moving information becomes, so that everyone in investing ends up knowing the same things at the same time and investing in the same vehicles. Finding the road less traveled has become a quixotic quest.

When you first go to a new broker, typically an uninformed shill for the financial products of his or her employer, here is how usually it works. Your adviser will divide your life savings into two buckets. One bucket is invested at the firm. The other bucket is handed to an outside manager, who supposedly is offering some terrific targeted stock-picking strategy when, in reality, it is just another form of mutual funds.

By pushing some of your money off to these outside managers, your adviser is removing liability from his firm and offloading it to this other firm, playing it safe with the other half of your account by investing in exchange-traded funds (ETFs) and using some variation of the standard asset allocation between stocks and bonds. That isn't nearly a wide enough span of investment types to lower your risk. You need to spread it out among many different baskets.

Building a well-constructed investment portfolio can be a lot more difficult than building a well-constructed dream house—and it can take a lot longer, too: three to five years, for starters. In fact, even five years is too short a time to evaluate a portfolio's real success or failure. *Ten years* is the ideal time span needed for you to conduct a truly comprehensive evaluation.

Here's a rather stunning fact on stock prices and ten-year periods: if you calculate stocks' total value at the start and end of every ten-year period for the past 200 years—from 1818 to 1828, 1819–29, 1820–30, and so on—that amounts to 200 ten-year spans. Of those 200 ten-year spans, stocks lost value only *once*. That exception was from 1927 to 1937, in the years encompassing the Great Depression.

So, if you and your ancestors faithfully followed buy-and-hold in stocks for the past 200 years, with a ten-year outlook at the least, over the generations you faced only one chance in 200 of losing money on stocks in a ten-year period. It is an extraordinary record.

These days, however, investors who practice truly long-term investing are an endangered species. Nobody talks in those terms anymore. Brokerage firms tout cheap trades and high-volume discounts to sign up fidgety-fingered day traders of stocks. CEOs obsess over three-month earnings reports rather than ten-year strategic plans. We hear buy-and-hold is dead, and shareholder loyalty has dissipated like the attention span of a smartphone addict.

CNBC, Fox Business Network, and Bloomberg follow the fluctuations in the prices of stocks, energy, precious metals, and bond yields on a minute-by-minute basis every day, though none of this has much to do with long-term investing. And long-term investing is the *only* kind of investing you should do.

Indeed, CNBC arguably is one of the worst things to happen to individual investors. To be on the air 24/7, CNBC had to make people think something mattered every moment. "This just in." People started worrying more about volatility and what the markets may do, and when they started using smartphones, they had the ability to push a few buttons and trade on their fears.

It is crazy how many ways a network can find to make viewers worry throughout the day—even if they aren't drinking coffee. Then Starbucks came along and made it worse. People who are nervous all day long become bad investors. There are bad investments and a hundred times more bad investors. People need a wall between themselves and their money. They need to understand why volatility is killing them.

Producing good television requires a heightened sense of action, while good investing is a bit like good fishing: shut up and wait. Though I run hundreds of millions of dollars of other people's money, until recently I rejected having a TV set in my office. I want to avoid distractions, and the daily frenzy and the bit-stream of headlines and price movements coming across CNBC and Fox Business Network are nothing but noise—*they don't count for anything.*

Warren Buffett might never have become the consummate long-term investor if CNBC had been on-air when he started trading. (Though, while others extoll the brilliance of the supposed Oracle of Omaha, my belief is that Buffett's biggest advantage in investing is simply his longevity—he turned eighty-seven in 2018; he has had abundant time for most of his investments to go up. Buy and hold, until you die.)

People err by responding to emotion, succumbing to fear, and trading when they should stand idle. The more you trade, the more wrong moves you can make. In the five-year period from1991 to 1996, the S&P 500 index of the 500 biggest companies rose 18 percent, and all the investor needed to do was buy shares in an S&P mutual fund and wait; in the same period, active traders posted a *decline* of 11.4 percent.

In the ten-year period leading up to the end of 2013, investors' actual returns lagged behind the returns in the assets they owned by 2.5 percentage points per year, according to a recent study published by the investment research firm Morningstar; in the ten years leading up to March 31, 2018, the average mutual fund gained 5.79 percent annually, while the average investor gained only 5.53 percent per year. This is because individual investors tend to buy high and sell low rather than the other way around, which itself is the aim of all investing.

We see this ill-fated fidgetiness in the shortening time frame for holding on to stocks before selling out. Investors held on to a stock for an average duration of twelve *years* in the 1950s. This holding period shrank to eight years in the 1960s, less than three years by 1980, only fourteen months by 2000, and just six months in 2010 (in the skittish aftermath of the Great Meltdown). In 2016, the average time for holding a stock was only four months. In 2018, it was all of eight months.

## What Really Counts

It is all too easy nowadays for an investor to lose track of what counts and get distracted by meaningless static that seems to be more important than it really is. Before the cable news channels dawned more than thirty years ago, news took a very long time to reach the retail investor.

Institutional investors had ample time to digest the news and decide what to do. The geopolitical global picture for investing evolved only slowly, decades ago. People were patient. They would wait for developments. Before they could trade out of a stock they owned, they had to reach their broker and discuss it, then put in a request and pay high fees.

At this slower pace of the old days, the major stock exchanges, blue-chip stocks, and the analysts at the big Wall Street firms all reacted to news first. Lagging behind them and reacting later were the less-studied backwaters of investing, including small-cap stocks, overseas international stocks, and emerging markets.

Because of this delay, these backwaters moved in ways different from the major markets. The small-cap and overseas stocks were uncorrelated to the market overall.

These alternative assets provided a safe haven for investors in US stocks. When stock prices plunged, the backwater markets fell less, held steady, or even rose in value because they hadn't reacted to the news yet.

Then came the cable business networks, covering stock prices from the floor of the New York Stock Exchange and turning investing into a televised sport. The velocity of news skyrocketed. It went into hyperspace mode with the rise of the internet, websites and blogs and podcasts, chatrooms, online bulletin boards, Facebook, Twitter, Instagram, and LinkedIn all fueling fickle and furious day trading by individual investors.

Now the stocks in small cap, emerging markets, overseas exchanges, and other backwaters that had been uncorrelated to the US markets react in sync with us; they are highly correlated to the markets. This is because they get their news so much faster. It takes only seconds for an isolated outbreak of E. coli at Chipotle or some other publicly traded restaurant chain to make the front-page screen of the Google newsfeed seen around the world all at once. Institutions and investors can react instantly, and they do, at times to their detriment.

Can we all just slow the heck down?

Take a look at the following chart. It shows how closely correlated each index was to others over different time periods. In comparing one index to another, a correlation of 1.00 means the two indexes trade exactly alike all the time, 100 percent correlation.

Jan. 1991 – Dec. 2001  /  Jan. 2002 – Dec. 2018

| | Russell 1000 Growth | Russell 1000 Value | S&P 500 | Russell 2000 Index | Emerging Markets | International Markets |
|---|---|---|---|---|---|---|
| **Russell 1000 Growth** | 1.00 | 0.57 / 0.93 | 0.90 / 0.98 | 0.47 / 0.91 | -0.06 / 0.89 | 0.24 / 0.85 |
| **Russell 1000 Value** | 0.57 / 0.93 | 1.00 | 0.87 / 0.98 | 0.57 / 0.94 | -0.12 / 0.88 | 0.17 / 0.91 |
| **S&P 500** | 0.90 / 0.98 | 0.87 / 0.98 | 1.00 | 0.50 / 0.95 | -0.15 / 0.90 | 0.24 / 0.91 |
| **Russell 2000 Index** | 0.47 / 0.91 | 0.57 / 0.94 | 0.50 / 0.95 | 1.00 | 0.44 / 0.84 | 0.29 / 0.89 |
| **Emerging Markets** | -0.06 / 0.74 | -0.12 / 0.74 | -0.15 / 0.90 | 0.44 / 0.75 | 1.00 | 0.41 / 0.89 |
| **International Markets** | 0.24 / 0.85 | 0.17 / 0.91 | 0.24 / 0.94 | 0.29 / 0.89 | 0.41 / 0.93 | 1.00 |

Less than half the time in the 1990s did the various indexes operate like one another; they shared less than 50 percent correlation. From 2000 to 2018, the correlation was at more than 90 percent. From 1990 to 2000, international markets had only a correlation of 0.24 to the S&P 500 index, which means that international mimicked big stocks only 24 percent of the time; that correlation was up to 0.85 from 2002 to 2018.

Emerging markets before 2000 had a correlation of less than zero compared with the S&P, at -0.15; that correlation is currently +0.90 or 90 percent.

## Coincidence of Correlation

Nowadays almost everything is 100 percent correlated to every other index; even alternative-focused hedge funds are very correlated to the stock market. And if all these indexes for all these different types of assets move in the same direction at the same time, where is an investor supposed to find a safe haven that will run counter to everything else?

The days are long gone when you might have had a truly diversified portfolio, as far as correlation goes. The more correlated your portfolio is to the overall market, the more volatility there is in your portfolio, and the more risk it carries. When the market goes up or down, your portfolio goes up or down right along with it.

The key to reducing risk is reducing volatility. In order to do this, you need to be invested primarily in assets that all have different correlations and which, preferably, aren't correlated to one another at all.

This is tricky stuff, and most pros fail at it. In the past fifteen years, according to a 2017 study by Standard & Poor's Corp., 92 percent of large-cap funds lagged behind a simple S&P 500 index fund, and managers of mid-caps and small-cap funds fared even worse, with 95 percent of mid-cap managers and 93 percent of small-cap managers trailing behind their benchmarks.

It is an embarrassment. Think about that. You are paying these people to manage your life savings, a lot of them charge 1 percent of your assets every year, and almost all of them fail to do any better than the benchmark ETF that you could buy on your own.

Large-cap *value* companies, just so you know, are giant blue chips worth $10 billion or more in total market value (market capitalization) whose stock price is lower than what it should be, given their underlying intrinsic value. So, their stocks are cheaper pound-for-pound and often pay a tidy dividend. Large-cap *growth* companies, by contrast, are giants that emphasize growth and expansion over dividends. They reinvest their earnings in building the business, hoping to lift the stock price to ensure capital appreciation for investors (and compensate for the lack of cash dividends).

Wealth managers who run international stock funds will compare their performance to the MSCI EAFE Index, which measures stocks' performance across twenty-one developed countries. It is a misleading metric, however, because it includes Japan, whose stock market has lain dormant for many years (and is at the level, value-wise, that it had held in the mid-1980s). Thus, that reduces the long-term performance of the entire overseas stock index, making it easier to outperform.

Why do so few managers outperform their benchmark indices? Some of it has to do with lack of training and talent. As we have seen, nobody understands how to measure risk, so how could any manager be expected to properly account for it in investments? Some of it has to do with the expectations that, if a manager runs a certain kind of fund, he is crazy not to have certain staples in his portfolio, even if they aren't good companies. A dividend-centric fund is expected to own stocks of blue chips that pay only modest dividends, even though a lot of them are extremely overvalued as I write this book.

Another factor in advisers' underperformance, however, is the lack of easily available non-correlated assets to help balance out the volatility in their clients' accounts. Until 1983, nobody deemed non-correlated assets to be an important aspect of investment strategy. Then a Harvard business professor named John Virgil Lintner delivered a landmark paper entitled "The Potential Role of Managed Commodity-Financial Futures Accounts (and/or Funds) in Portfolios of Stocks and Bonds." Not exactly a sexy title, and it is as complicated as it sounds.

Lintner's bottom line was that portfolios of stocks and/or bonds, combined with non-correlated investments called managed futures, showed substantially less risk at every possible level of expected returns than stocks and/or bonds alone. As he put it:

> *"Indeed...the correlations between the returns on the futures portfolios and those on the stock and bond portfolios are [so] surprisingly low (sometimes even negative)—that the return/risk trade-offs provided by augmented portfolios...clearly dominate the trade-offs available from portfolios of stocks alone."*

He adds: "Moreover, they do so by very considerable margins." These combined portfolios of stocks, bonds, and managed futures "show substantially less risk at every possible level of expected return than portfolios of stock alone (or from portfolios of stocks and bonds)." Then, Lintner dismounts and sticks the landing: "Finally, all the above conclusions continue to hold when returns are measured in real as well as in nominal terms, and also when returns are adjusted for the risk-free rate on Treasury bills."

This was groundbreaking work, and it shocked the industry. This theory has expanded to include many different types of non-correlated investments and securities. Coming up in the next chapter, we take a closer look at this gang of contrarians, starting with my list of the most non-correlated assets that every investor should consider adding to his or her portfolio.

# CHAPTER 8

# Non-Correlated Assets

In the hunt for a different breed of assets that are unaffected by the gyrations in the stock market, you must be willing to go beyond the normal boundaries of publicly traded securities, all of which trade alike these days. Making the quest even more difficult, you must find myriad different kinds of investments and combine them. None of these rare, contrarian assets can stand alone; any one investment by itself is inadequate.

Let us start with eight categories that are among the most non-correlated assets of all.

### Hard Money Loans

While giant companies go to the equity and bond markets to raise money, small businesses and individual investors in need of cash often must turn to local sources. Therein looms a great return for those who have the capital to offer loans. Plus, these direct loans have virtually no correlation at all to the stock market. My fund recently made a $4.5 million loan to a well-paid relief pitcher for a legendary team in Major

League Baseball, at 14 percent annual interest plus a 1 percent fee up front. The league sends his biweekly paycheck to my firm until we are paid back in full.

## Factoring

Cash flow is the lifeblood of business, and the biggest businesses hold on to their cash as long as possible before paying their bills, delaying payment until thirty, sixty, or ninety days after they received the services or products from the usually smaller businesses that served them. That offers a 20 percent profit your money can make, rather easily, on factoring.

Factoring entails buying a stream of income at a discount of 10–20 percent, paying cash *now* for a business's receivables and collecting the payments as they arrive *later*. The risk may be too high for some investors because companies seeking factoring sometimes have cash-flow weaknesses that can impair their ability to repay the debt they just added to their balance sheets. Yet factoring is one of the few small corners left in investing in which the actual risk of a loss turns out to be far lower than perceived and, therefore, the premium is commensurately higher.

Say a business is owed $1 million by a bigger, cash-stingy customer; for $800,000 in cash up front, the business hands over the bill to the factor, who collects the $1 million payment and pockets the $200,000 upside: a 20 percent profit in weeks.

In Texas the electricity market is deregulated, and my firm engages in factoring for companies in the industry to the tune of $1 million a month and a 20 percent profit. We built in a possible default rate of 15 percent and still would have made money. Thus far, we have gone default-free, low-risk, and high-return—and utterly non-correlated to the markets for all kinds of publicly traded securities.

In another arrangement, this one with a lingerie brand that can't afford to wait forty to sixty days to be paid by apparel retailers, we pay

$160,000 to acquire $200,000 a month in receivables, clearing $40,000 a month.

If you can make even a 10 percent profit per month, that is a 120 percent return on your money in a year. At first glance it may seem unwise for any business to pay a 10 percent fee for up-front cash, yet an apparel business with 45 percent margins will happily pay ten percentage points to get cash now and invest it back in the business, so it can supply more orders. Never have I sought out a factoring agreement; they keep coming to me via my clients.

## Diamonds

Diamonds are forever, as James Bond realized, and diamonds also can be a great investment. Diamond prices go up and down with prices of gold, silver, iron ore, and other commodities. Best of all, you can get them at a discount. Despite ample price transparency thanks to guides such as the Rapp List, you can get them at a discount of up to 40 percent off current prices. This is because diamonds trade on private exchanges, while gold and silver trade on public exchanges. Be sure to buy only diamonds certified by the GIA (Gemological Institute of America) and no one else.

Also, diamonds are a phenomenal counterweight against the stock market, their prices having nothing to do with stock prices. The risk is that diamonds may be hard to sell in panicky times, and prices could fall; that risk in actuality is low, though, because few people want to sell diamonds in a crash.

## Gold and Silver

Better yet, let's call it Silver and Gold, for silver is the better investment, in my view. Gold is so heavily traded that no wiggle room exists to allow discounts or offer an easy way to make a fast buck. When gold is at $1,285 an ounce, you will pay $1,285. Period. No matter where you buy it. Silver, always second banana to gold, may have more leeway for an upside surprise.

Gold prices, especially, can soar when the prices of stocks and bonds plunge in a financial meltdown, as investors seek solace in a truly precious metal prized by mankind for four thousand years. Gold has always been in short supply and is so difficult to unearth. Fun fact: if you combined all the gold accumulated worldwide since the Egyptians began mining it in 2000 BC, how many Olympic-sized swimming pools would it fill up?

Answer: Three and a third, as *Forbes* calculated some years ago. (Or 3.27 pools at 2.5 million liters of capacity per pool, to be precise.) That is precious.

## Private Equity and Venture Capital

Happily both private equity (PE) and venture capital (VC) are entirely non-correlated to the movements in the stock market. Unhappily, both are an easy way to lose your shirt. I have seen plenty of money lost in private equity funds, and keep in mind that in venture capital, only one in thirty investments actually turns into a home run. My advice to clients is generally to avoid putting money into these two sectors unless they first have accumulated more than $3 million in their portfolios.

Private equity can invest in companies of various sizes, even huge ones, and at various stages, even twenty or thirty years after their founding; while venture capital focuses on early stages of a business, sometimes just an idea. In public-markets investing, my goal is to double your money in a bit longer than seven years (7.2 years, to be precise), which is what will happen if we can get consistent returns of 10 percent a year. In private equity, investors should be looking to double (or triple) their money in five years, in my view. In venture capital, you should assume every penny you invest will be lost, while looking to make ten times your money in seven to ten years.

## Emerging Markets Debt

Very non-correlated to the US markets, emerging-market debt can go up in price in bad times in the US. Conversely, this also is why this form of debt has been losing money in 2018, when US stocks kept rising to new, record-high levels. This category includes fixed-income debt or bonds issued in the international debt market by governments, agencies, and corporations in developing countries. As early as the 1970s, multinational banks in the US and Europe were issuing bonds for developing countries, especially in Latin America. Since then, the industry has grown to allow investments from both individual and institutional investors.

Investors can buy emerging market debt via mutual funds offered by Pimco, Vanguard, Western Asset Management, Alliance Bernstein, and others. The funds are run by professional portfolio managers and tend to offer higher returns than other debt instruments, due to the higher level of risk they carry. This asset class was hot in 2017, but be careful about whether a bond pays out in US dollars or a more volatile currency.

## Real Estate Investment Trusts (REITs)

It may sound like an inheritance for Richie Rich, "the poor little rich boy" of 1950s comic book fame, but the REIT is an easily accessible vehicle that lets investors own a piece of the ongoing income from a portfolio of properties such as restaurants and office buildings. Though REITs are publicly traded securities, they still trade in ways that run counter to stock trends, which makes them a nicely non-correlated outlet.

You will recall reading earlier that after I was fired from my first job out of college, I moved into a public-storage building in Austin for a few months. So it may strike you as funny, or fitting, that today I hold a special affection for a class of REITs based on rents collected from public-storage units.

They are among the best REITS you can buy, and better yet they are a world away from stocks and utterly non-correlated to the markets' rise and fall. Public storage companies boast the upside of rising real estate values of the properties they own, they churn out steady income, and they provide a service that will always be necessary. People need to store things all the time; we run out of room.

REITs invest in mortgages, buy and develop properties, and maintain their ownership to collect rents as part of the investment portfolio for long-term income. Just as with equities, investors acquire ownership in REITs through stock ownership. Most REITs are traded on a stock exchange, and investors can buy their stock online or through a broker.

Some REITs are privately held, and you still can buy them through a broker who participates in their offerings. The SEC regulates publicly traded and non-traded REITs. Another way investors can invest in REITs is through mutual funds and ETFs.

Public REITs must disclose all details of their financial performance, while private REITs are just that, permitted to keep all details private—a key reason I never buy into a private REIT. Disclosure of information gives the investor more control. Plus, when you buy a private REIT, you are unable to sell it into the market, generally; usually you are required to sell your shares back to the REIT company at the price it dictates, or you must find someone specific to buy it from you.

While REITs offer investors a simple opportunity to include real estate in their portfolios without having to buy physical properties, they have drawbacks, especially the non-traded REITs. The latter can cost you a 10 percent fee up front, and they are illiquid and hard to sell quickly to raise cash. Plus, it is difficult to peg the real value of a non-traded REIT stock; these hassles are why non-traded REITs usually pay a higher dividend yield than publicly traded REITs. Also, REITS pay out 90 percent of their income to their shareholders, so you will take a tax hit on what you receive, which can be a shocker.

## Preferred Stocks

A preferred stock, though it can trade similarly to the common stock in the same company, has a low correlation with the broad stock market overall, and it is uncorrelated with traditional fixed income as well.

Unlike ordinary shares of stock, preferred stocks pay fixed dividends to investors irrespective of whether the company makes a profit, and these dividends usually are higher than the dividends paid on common shares. If the company falters, preferred shareholders get paid before common shareholders, although both kinds of shareholders get paid only after bondholders and other creditors are made whole.

Preferred stock can trade publicly in the way that common stock trades, but it can also receive agency ratings just as bonds do. Preferred shares also are less volatile and have higher yields than most other asset classes.

\* \* \*

Those are eight kinds of the most non-correlated assets worth weighing for your portfolio. Now, we review still more possibilities and some more exotic plays. The striking truth is that many of these high-risk, intricately sophisticated methods are available to rank-and-file investors via dedicated mutual funds and ETFs.

## Managed Futures

Managed futures have a very low correlation to traditional investments, ensuring stability when added to a portfolio that already includes stocks, bonds, and real estate. The tricky part for the adviser is to determine the investor's comfort level for risk.

A key difference separates *managed* futures from regular futures contracts. In regular futures contracts, your losses can multiply wildly and extend even beyond the amount you invested, while *managed* futures can limit your losses to 100 percent of what you put at risk.

Managed futures involve professional fund managers running entire portfolios of hundreds or thousands of futures contracts and sifting among their spreads and price fluctuations.

Futures contracts are the right to buy or sell a given commodity at some point in the future, at a price we agree upon today; the contract itself trades publicly and can go up or down in price in far wilder swings than what the underlying prices undergo.

Let's say Apple stock is trading at $185 and you think it will exceed $200 in less than three months. Buy the stock now and if you turn out to be right, you have made fifteen dollars a share, up 8 percent. Far bigger gains, however, can be made on a futures contract that gives you the right to buy a thousand shares of Apple three months from now at that same $185. The contract is worthless today because you can buy the stock for $185, but if Apple rises to $200, then the contract to buy it at $185 is suddenly worth several times your original cost. Now it's in the money; sell it and your returns are far higher than 8 percent.

Airlines buy contracts like this for jet fuel to hedge against sudden price increases that would crush their profit margins. Farmers use futures to offset bad prices for corn and soybeans. The main purpose of futures contracts, though, is for betting and hedging and speculating at the highest levels of sophisticated investing.

## Commodities

Commodities are the components and building blocks of other products and other industries, and they act as both an economic indicator for where the economy might be heading and a target for investment and speculation via the futures markets. Examples include precious metals, pork bellies, beef, oil, grains, natural gas, electricity, and foreign exchange currencies.

Commodities and stock prices tend to move in opposite directions, so commodities are a must-have in constructing a balanced investment portfolio. However, commodities can be much more volatile than stocks, and therefore the investor must be careful to limit exposure to a safe level.

Investors can trade commodities through the spot market or the futures market. In the spot market, the buyer and the seller complete their transaction on the spot based on current market prices. The futures market, by contrast, involves a transaction by which the buyer and the seller agree to deliver the underlying commodity in the future at a price set now. Consequently, the buyer avoids the risk of rising prices while the seller avoids the risk of falling prices.

Futures were initially used to help farmers and ranchers do business. While they are still used that way, they have also become a massive gambling instrument for traders betting on price movements. More than 90 percent of these contracts never result in any real transactions; it is all invisible gains and losses when contracts soar in value or plummet or expire.

Commodity futures trading is regulated by the Commodity Futures Trading Commission (CFTC) through the 1974 Commodity Exchange Act. The role of the CFTC includes ensuring competitiveness, efficiency, and integrity in the market and preventing fraud. Investors can get into the commodities market by buying through index funds, mutual funds or ETFs that invest in companies that deal with commodities. Investors also can buy futures directly from commodity exchanges, or they can purchase stock in companies that rely on commodities prices.

Some of the most popular commodity exchanges in the US include the Chicago Board of Trade (CBOT), the Chicago Board Options Exchange (now Cboe), and the New York Mercantile Exchange (Nymex). The Nymex is the biggest physical commodity futures exchange in the world.

### Arbitrage: Convertible, Fixed Income, Merger

Three major kinds of betting make up the art of arbitrage, and these investments are an absolutely great counterweight to stocks in terms of non-correlation. *Convertible Arbitrage* is a market-neutral hedge fund strategy that involves betting for and against a company at the same time. Simultaneously, you purchase convertible securities issued by the company (convertible into company shares of stock) and you sell the company's stock short, betting it will decline in value.

This works well when the convertible is priced inefficiently relative to the underlying stock, letting arbitrage traders profit on the price gaps between the two. The best plans, however, can go awry in this strategy.

In 2005 many arbitrageurs sold General Motors shares short. That is, they sold borrowed shares in a bet the stock price would plunge, letting them step in later and buy the now-cheaper shares to cover their bet and pay back the borrowed stock they had sold. These traders simultaneously bought GM convertible bonds. They got crushed when the ratings agencies issued a surprise downgrade of GM bonds, sending their price tumbling. Then some big bond investors switched to GM stock and that sent the price higher, clobbering traders on their bet that GM stock would fall. A one-two punch.

*Fixed Income Arbitrage* involves debt instruments issued to raise money in return for paying out periodic coupons to the lenders, then returning all principal at maturity of the debt. They include treasuries, bonds, commercial paper, certificates of deposit, and interest rate swaps. Hedge funds seek to exploit the pricing differences among these various investment vehicles.

Say a five-year bond with 4 percent interest is selling at $105.50 in one market and at $104.40 in the other—a gap or spread of $1.10. An arb can buy in the cheaper market and sell in the higher one, pocketing the difference; computer algorithms handle this kind of transaction hundreds and thousands of times a day. This is for real pros.

*Merger Arbitrage* seeks to take advantage of stock pricing differentials smack in the middle of merger talks. The recent Disney-Fox-Comcast takeover battle offered the arbs abundant opportunities to surf back and forth among the media stocks, as Disney thought it had locked up a deal to buy key Fox assets, then pulled the surprise of pre-empting Comcast with a significantly higher bid—even though Comcast hadn't revealed any bid as yet. The stock price of the company doing the acquisition tends to fall upon a deal's unveiling, and the stock of the company getting bought tends to rise, sometimes sharply. In that volatility, the arbs mine for gold.

## Master Limited Partnership (MLP)

An MLP refers to a limited partnership that is publicly traded on a stock exchange. A limited partnership is a business structure that consists of a general partner and a limited partner. General partners are personally liable for all debts and obligations of business, while limited partners are liable only to the extent of their investment. Limited partnerships have a tax advantage since their income is not taxed at the business level.

An MLP combines both the tax advantages of a limited partnership and the liquidity of the stock market. Just like REITs, MLPs are required by law to pay the biggest portion of their earnings to their partners. The limited partners are the shareholders, who should, therefore, receive a return in proportion to their investment.

Investors can buy limited partnership units the same way they buy stocks through a broker. MLPs pay investors quarterly required distributions (QRDs), which are in many ways different from the dividends paid by stocks. Unlike dividends, QRDs are mandatory, meaning that a missed payment constitutes a default. MLPs must, therefore, ensure they have steady cash flows to be able to meet the required payments to shareholders.

Since MLPs are not taxed at the business level, the shareholders have a duty to remit their income tax after receiving their share of income. Investors in low-income tax brackets (such as well-off retirees) can enjoy higher returns in MLPs than in stocks, where taxation happens both at the business level and at the individual level. That is, a publicly held company pays corporate income tax on the profit it makes, after which it pays cash dividends to its shareholders—who then must pay a second tax on that dividend income. Double taxation. Investors also can include MLPs in their portfolio through mutual funds and ETFs that invest in them.

## Business Development Companies (BDC)

A BDC is a firm that invests in Small and Medium Enterprises (SMEs) in their initial stages of growth. A small-biz angel. It is a closed-end investment company that helps up-and-coming businesses meet their capital requirements and grow.

Interestingly, most BDCs are publicly traded and attract a large number of investors due to their high yields. The high yields are the tradeoff for the risk involved in investing in small and medium enterprises.

BDCs make money for investors by providing capital and skills to SMEs in exchange for stock and income from debt. They are similar to venture capital funds but are open to all investors. BDCs distribute 90 percent or more of their income to their shareholders every year, though the tax treatment is more favorable for investors. Taxes are paid only at the individual level rather than at both the individual and corporate levels.

This asset class requires an investor's courage in uncertain, crisis-prone patches because it uses lots of leverage (investing one dollar and borrowing five dollars more to invest in the same thing), and while this magnifies income in good times, it amplifies losses in bad times. Also, the use of debt capital in BDCs makes them a risky bet in an environment of rising interest rates...say, right about now.

## Long/Short Equity

This strategy involves buying stocks you expect to rise in value over a relatively longer period, and also short-selling weak stocks you expect to stumble in the short term. To sell a stock short, the investor borrows shares he doesn't yet own and promises to pay back the shares later. Then he sells those shares into the market at today's price and pockets the proceeds. He waits for the price to nosedive, and once the stock has lost ample value, the seller then buys the now-cheaper shares on the open market, pays them back to the broker that had loaned out the original shares, and his profit is the difference.

The risk can be huge, though, if the stock price rises and the short seller ends up having to cover his bet by buying richer shares to pay them back, thereby taking a big loss. Short sellers have lost hundreds of millions of dollars betting against the unlikely success of Tesla and its $50,000 electric (and electrifying) sports cars.

In the Long/Short Equity strategy, the trader enters a long and short position simultaneously in the same industry to acquire a market neutral position. A bold investor might make a $2 million bet on Tesla stock, paying for it with $2 million he picked up by short-selling Ferrari shares in a bet that Ferrari stock will go down in price. If auto sales falter and all carmakers' shares plummet, the loss on Tesla shares will be canceled out by the short position gain on Ferrari shares. Likewise, if the industry performs well and both stocks rise, the Tesla upside will defray losses on the Ferrari short.

In a related strategy known as *Dedicated Short Bias,* hedge funds use similar tactics and focus their efforts predominately on the bet-against-them short side.

## Event Driven

Even in the overly wired-up world of today, fast-breaking, sudden events can cause a firm's stock to be priced wrong over the short-term. Investing at these moments is the centerpiece of the event driven approach. A surprise corporate bankruptcy filing, a company restructuring, a merger or acquisition, even a testy earnings call, all can set a company's stock reeling. And traders thrive on that kind of volatility.

They also can lose tons of money by betting in the wrong direction on the same thing.

## Money Market Funds

The money market fund is one of the safest, cheapest, dullest ways to park your cash—it *is* cash, pretty much. Whether stock prices are roaring up or taking a dive, money markets hold their value and stay put. They are the main source of short-term cash to cover "liquidity needs" for governments, financial institutions, and companies. Money markets are open to institutional investors and retail investors. For retail investors, money market mutual funds offer a slightly higher return than fixed deposits, not to mention their high liquidity (their ability to produce your cash quickly), although they inevitably trail behind the real COLA in your life.

Another advantage of money markets is that they are managed by a professional and regulated by the SEC. Money markets attract investors in times of high global investment uncertainty. This is because they are largely risk-free and highly liquid. In times of extreme global uncertainty as in the Great Meltdown of 2008, however, the level of risk in money markets can rise dramatically; then again, chances are the risk will be higher still for most everything else.

In the Great Meltdown, one much-watched money market fund took the rare tumble of "breaking the buck," falling below the one-dollar-a-share level that is a money-market mainstay. To prevent a run on money markets that could have dried up liquidity and added to the sense of crisis around the globe, the US government stepped up and assured investors that all money market funds would be backed by government support. This stopped further volatility and offered investors a clue that in the next meltdown, money markets have all but an explicit government guarantee.

# CHAPTER 9

# The Skinny on Bonds

Having read the preceding list of non-correlated alternative investments and arbitrage plays in chapters seven and eight, you now may have spent more time studying portfolio construction than most advisers on Wall Street. All portfolios should have some contrarian, against-the-grain assets that run counter to the broader trend.

This chapter is devoted to one of the vastest and most diverse asset classes: bonds. They come in an astonishing array of shapes and sizes and durations, not to mention issuers, yet all of them share some underlying traits and risks.

Insisting all portfolios should own some bonds is a dubious proposition. The fact is, I don't like bonds very much, and a lot of portfolios can do just fine without them. I rarely buy them, the exception being Dr. Pepper and Colt .45 high-yield bonds in the early '90s. One study of the biggest endowments and pension funds found that bonds occupied only 7 percent of their portfolios.

The idea people have that bonds are *safe* bothers me. Safe from what? Safe from capital loss, okay, but they have plenty of risks of their own, and the largest risk is the loss of purchasing power. That is the most unforgivable flaw of bonds: they fail to keep up with your COLA and the rising prices in your life. That flaw deeply offends me, I cannot help it; it makes me think of my late mother and her struggles to keep up with inflation at the end of her life.

Municipal bonds and government bonds are the biggest laggards in this regard. My advice to clients is that they never should buy Treasury notes of one-year, two-year or three-year durations—they are certain to lose ground to the rising cost of living; same goes for a thirty-year government bond.

Bond yields and rates track the rising prices as measured by the Consumer Price Index, because the higher the rate of inflation in the economy, the higher the interest rates that borrowers must pay to make the promised returns attractive. If you buy a one-year Treasury bill paying a 5 percent interest rate, and a year later the going rate is 6 percent, your bill is worth less. If you buy a thirty-year government bond and hold it to maturity, you will have lost a startling amount of purchasing power in that time.

It is clear that stocks outperform bonds over the long term; bonds are an okay non-correlated counterbalance, an afterthought to cushion the ups and downs of the equities that anchor a portfolio.

The Wharton finance professor Jeremy Siegel studied the prices of stocks, Treasury bonds, T-Bills, gold, and the US dollar from 1802 to 2012. How's that for long term? In those 210 years, stocks had average annual returns of 6.5 percent, Treasury bonds (with durations of two, three, and five years) had half that return at 3.3 percent, and T-Bills (bonds lasting less than a year) had an even lower annual return of 2.7 percent after adjusting for inflation.

That gap between stocks' superior performance and bonds' poky pace is even bigger than it looks, compounding over the decades into a huge windfall in higher returns for the owner of stocks. Siegel also found that stocks are less risky than government bonds for holding periods of twenty years or longer, after adjusting for inflation.

Recall also that in the fifteen years leading up to year-end 2011, ten-year Treasury bonds kept pace with inflation less than 20 percent of the time, and investors were down 25 percent in purchasing power by the end of that period.

Given government bonds' lackluster returns and their failure to maintain full purchasing power amid rising prices, perhaps corporate bonds offer a better alternative. Just one problem: corporate bonds, those of the highest quality, trade like government bonds and also lose pace to inflation because of the low interest rates they pay. I'm talking about corporates with a credit rating of single-A or higher.

Corporate bonds at the double-B level or weaker are an entirely different beast, and these distressed bonds pay significantly higher rates to compensate for their supposedly higher risk of default, which can be overstated even in these days of hyper-connected information flow.

If you own bonds rated triple-B or higher, you have what is known as bank credit, and the bonds are affected, for the most part, by the rise or fall in interest rates in the broader economy. That's it. Put money into lower-rated double-B bonds or worse, and changes in interest rates have very little impact on them; the main issue is the credit quality of the company and how strong its balance sheet is.

Despite my misgivings about bonds, one good thing about them is their due date, whatever it may be. Whether it is a mere three-month Treasury bill or a two-year note or a thirty-year bond or something in between, the contractually committed promise to repay you on a particular date of maturity is an extra measure of safety.

That is the good news. The surprising exception is that, while buying a bond is investing in *debt*, when you invest in a bond *fund* (a basket of dozens or hundreds of bonds of various issuers, types, durations, interest rates, and terms), you aren't investing in debt and bonds at all. Instead, a stake in a bond fund is an investment in *equity*, like a stock is equity, because you essentially are buying shares in a bond fund owned by a company, which itself is the owner of the individual bonds.

A bond fund has no maturity date, no guaranteed payback by an agreed upon deadline. Therefore any extra measure of safety offered by bonds themselves is absent when they all are cobbled together in a broad fund supposedly aimed at reducing the risks of owning any one bond.

Also, while you shop for bonds mainly by looking at the interest rates their issuers pledge to pay, the real thing to watch is the fluctuating prices of bonds in response to interest-rate movements, economic conditions, crisis headlines, and the like. In 1994, most bond funds lost a jarring 19 percent of their value in a single year because most bonds are sensitive to interest rates, and rates were on the rise. Yet bonds supposedly are less volatile investments than stocks.

The original buyers of bonds typically sell them off before the bonds reach maturity, to pocket profits if possible and reinvest them in the next round of bonds at the latest interest rates. In a crisis, a US Treasury bond is especially non-correlated to the stock market. The bond can surge up in price, letting the owner take profits by selling to the next buyer; the next buyer is willing to receive the lower effective interest rate that results from the higher price he just paid to grab on to something *safe*.

Though bonds can be a losing option, nonetheless I discuss their types, risks, and upsides in the rundown that follows. Before an investor shuns any particular investment, it is important to understand what he or she is shunning. Let us begin with one of the biggest categories of all.

## Government Bonds

Bonds are debt securities issued by governments, utilities, school districts, companies, and the like. An investor puts up, say, $100,000 to buy a bond from the issuer. The issuer pays interest on that debt, at a set rate in quarterly or biannual installments, until the bond comes due (reaches maturity). Then the issuer must pay back the entire original sum to whoever holds the bond, based on the $100,000 face amount of the bond when it was issued.

Once a bond is floated, it can trade on the open market at fluctuating prices. If buyers seeking safety bid up the price of the $100,000 bond paying 2 percent interest so that the price suddenly jumps 10 percent to $110,000, its interest rate now pays only 1.8 percent to the new buyer. This is because the bond continues paying the same old rate of $2,000-a-year in interest, which now amounts to only 1.8 percent of the now-higher purchase price of the bond).

This is why bonds and interest rates are said to have an inverse relationship: when a bond's price rises and it gets sold to the next buyer, the effective interest rate it pays is suddenly lower than originally promised. When bond prices fall, the pre-set interest rates they pay increase commensurately, in terms of their new yield.

Moreover, existing bonds must compete for investors' capital with newly created government bonds paying the latest interest rates. After years of straitjacketing by the Federal Reserve, interest rates currently are rising, so each new batch of bonds may offer higher rates. This would depress the price of existing bonds paying a lower rate, causing investor losses for those who sell their old bonds at lower prices than they paid for them originally.

The US government is one of the most prodigious bond issuers on the planet. Treasury *bills* cover terms of less than a year, *notes* are issued in two-year, three-year, five-year, and ten-year increments, and Treasury *bonds* are thirty-year instruments that were reintroduced in 2006. The shorthand bonds is a catchall for all of the above.

Keep in mind that the supply of US bonds is unending and inelastic, because our government—past, present, and future—spends so much more than it takes in from tax collections. The US government spends hundreds of billions of dollars more every year than taxes haul in, and it covers this shortfall by selling bonds.

This overspending constitutes the annual budget deficit. We cover this shortfall by raising money from bond investors; thus, each budget year's *deficit* and the bonds the US sells to cover it add to the long-term national *debt* owed by the US government.

For decades, spending by the federal government has occupied an average of 21 percent of our national GDP, yet tax collections amounted to only 18 percent of GDP on average (with a low of 14 percent in the meltdown of 2008-09). The annual deficit hit the trillion-dollar mark for the first time in fiscal 2009 and stayed above that level for four years, declining to $438 billion in fiscal 2015; in fiscal 2019 it is estimated to exceed $980 billion.

To cover this gap, Congress charges it to the government's credit card. It lifts the debt limit so that the US Treasury can issue new government bonds to raise money now, promising to pay interest on it until we repay the entire principal. Usually, government pays back the old bonds by selling more new bonds and accumulating more debt. This borrowing to cover each year's deficit adds to the accumulating mountain of loans the government eventually must repay. If ever the US were to default on its bond payments, it might trigger a worldwide panic spreading at the light speed of fiber optics.

The result of this chronic overspending was $10 trillion in debt owed to bond investors by the federal government, racked up from the birth of our nation until 2008 at the end of eight years of George W. Bush and the wars in Afghanistan and Iraq. In just one decade since then, we have *doubled* the national debt, adding $10 trillion more to hit the $20 trillion mark. It is a staggering amount, equal to 100 percent of GDP.

Worse, we raised a lot of that money by borrowing from countries that compete with us or outright hate us (by selling them US government bonds). China is said to own close to $2 trillion in US bonds and other US-based assets. That hefty stake might look like some kind of chokehold on America, yet one is reminded of an old line attributed to the billionaire J. Paul Getty: "When you owe the bank $100 that's your problem. If you owe the bank $100 million, that's the bank's problem."

Thus, China's massive investment in US debt and other things American neutralizes it as an existential threat to us. We owe the Chinese government so much money in US bond obligations that China cannot afford to nuke its own assets. So, there's that.

Government bonds can be a good hedge against plunging stock prices. When stocks began tumbling in a rapidly spreading virus of fear in the Great Meltdown of 2008, institutional investors pulled out of stocks and corporate bonds in a flurry and funneled the money into Treasury bonds. This panic sent the price of ten-year Treasuries shooting higher, which further reduced their effective interest rate.

In July 2007, before the troubles started, ten-year Treasurys were yielding more than 5 percent annual interest. The rate plunged by more than half, to 2.16 percent, by December 2008, with the crisis fully raging after the collapse of Lehman Brothers.

The ten-year Treasury bond surged to almost 3.9 percent by August 2009 but fell back below 2 percent in 2011, tamped down by the Federal Reserve's aggressive bond-buying program, Quantitative Easing. QE aimed to create more demand for bonds to bid up their prices and thereby tamp down interest rates, and by 2012 the ten-year rate was back down to less than 1.7 percent. QE ended in October 2014, and by the summer of 2018, the ten-year rate was back up to almost 3 percent.

In the meltdown, investors were willing to take a much lower return on government bonds (meaning a lower interest rate) to have the assurance their money was safe. The US government remains the best bet to pay them back because if it ever runs out of money to make its loan payments, it can always avoid a default by revving up the printing presses to cover the obligation. This would, of course, trigger an onslaught of inflation; the surge of new money into the economy would find new uses, driving up prices.

While US government bonds are seen as having the lowest risk since they are backed by the full faith and credit of the US government (he said, whistling past the graveyard), other governments have a higher risk of default, especially those in developing countries. Ecuador, Grenada, Argentina, Indonesia, Pakistan, and, most recently, Venezuela, all have defaulted on their debt in years past.

Now, almost a decade after the Great Meltdown, the US economy is much stronger under President Trump, whether you like him or hate him (and there seems to be no in-between). Investors are bolder, betting on more risk rather than less, and the ten-year Treasury rates reflect this preference.

The Trump Rally sent stocks up strongly after his election in November 2016. On Election Day, the Dow Jones Industrial Average was at 18,332. By the end of January 2018, the index was up to 26,616, an astounding 45 percent in fifteen months, and the ten-year Treasury bond was at 2.66 percent, up from 2.15 percent in early November 2016. In the following year, the Dow average fell as low 22,445 and by early 2019 was back near the 26,000 mark.

While the federal government issues federal bonds, states, cities, towns, and local utilities issue municipal bonds. Investors can buy government bonds directly from the US Treasury or through a bank, dealer, or broker. For small investors, mutual funds offer an easy way to invest in government bonds.

As is true for all government bonds, inflation is a key investment risk. As inflation goes up, investors risk losing purchasing power. You can eliminate this downside by investing in inflation-indexed bonds. Another risk of bonds is that rising interest rates elsewhere will make their lower rates less attractive, and so their price will take a tumble, hurting their holders if they sell at the lower prices.

## Other Kinds of Bonds

*Corporate bonds* are issued by companies looking to raise new money now in exchange for slow, steady interest payments that can go on for anywhere from one to one-hundred years. The interest paid on a corporate bond can come in four flavors: fixed, floating, zero coupon, or adjustable. Fixed will pay you the promised rate until the bond finishes its run and comes due.

Floating rate corporate notes are preferable in times of rising interest rates because the interest rate they pay resets and rises with the rest of the market. Technically, these notes are direct loans rather than full-fledged bonds that are sold and traded on the public markets. Floating notes base their changing rate on LIBOR (an international interest rate among giant banks) or the Federal Funds Rate (the base rate on banks' overnight lending to one another, set by the US Federal Reserve) or some other formal reference point.

Zero coupon bonds, unlike the fixed and floating corporate bonds, pay no interest at all; instead, you buy them up front at a discount to their face value and receive the higher face amount at the end of the term. The gap between what you paid and what you received is your de facto interest rate.

Intriguing example: In 1984 quarterback Steve Young spurned the NFL draft to join the new USFL football league. The LA Express signed him to a $40 million contract—to be paid over forty-three years. The team paid him a $4 million bonus up front (vs. $1 million offered by the NFL's Cincinnati Bengals), plus less than $1 million in salary in four years. The remaining $30-some million was to be paid in the ensuing thirty-seven years, even if he left the team. That is one heck of a zero coupon bond. The deal with the USFL went kaput one year later, and Young pocketed $4.8 million and signed with the NFL's Tampa Bay Buccaneers.

Wall Street is especially inventive in crafting hundreds of different ways to do the same thing (raise capital), generating fees on all of

108

them. Thus corporate bonds come in many varieties. They can be callable or non-callable. Callable bonds let a company redeem them before they mature, therefore paying a higher rate than non-callable bonds to compensate for any chance of a surprise call-in.

You also can invest in convertible bonds that can be exchanged for company stock, although this makes convertibles vulnerable to stock-price movements, and usually we want bonds to offset stock risk rather than be affected adversely by it.

Bonds also can be investment grade or below (non-investment grade), based on credit-worthiness ratings issued by firms such as Moody's, Standard & Poor's, and Fitch. This is where bonds, so staid and colorless, suddenly get sexy.

The non-investment grade corporate bonds pay a significantly higher rate than the blue chips to compensate investors for being willing to take on a higher risk that the companies might falter and default on their bond obligations.

In the 1980s, Michael Milken and his bankers and traders at the old Drexel Burnham Lambert figured out a secret before everyone else— that these lower-rated bonds, disregarded by investors and therefore having to pay much richer rates, actually were far less likely to default than feared. This made them a deceptively attractive investment vehicle. Investors could reap double-digit returns on bonds that defaulted less frequently than conventional wisdom held.

Thus the "junk bond" boom was born, financing the 1980s takeover frenzy that saw high-yield bonds finance the leveraged buyouts, takeovers, and empire-building of RJR Nabisco, Revlon, MCI, Turner Broadcasting, Fox Television, Phillips Petroleum, Union Carbide, Federated Stores, Beatrice Cos., and Safeway, among many others.

Wall Street loves a good nickname like junk bonds, although practitioners prefer the term high-yield bonds. They traverse in a limited alphabet of bond ratings, below the august AAA corporations at the top, and even below the rungs of B and BB. In line with S&P and Fitch ratings, high-yield bonds are those below the BBB rating, even down to C and D, representing the lowest-grade junk.

Investors can get exposure to high-yield bonds through individual bonds, although mutual funds and exchange-traded funds are a better doorway for retail investors because the bonds are managed by professionals. By Moody's reckoning, the historical annual default rate on high-yield bonds currently stands at 4 percent, so 96 percent of the time you can be confident of avoiding any default.

In high-yield, the bigger risk is that volatility in the bonds' pricing can crush your capital, particularly in times of increased global uncertainty. The reason for this is that companies with a low credit rating find it much more difficult to secure financing in a crisis, when lenders have a greater fear of getting stiffed. This uncertainty can trigger a sell-off of high-yield bonds, making matters worse.

Elsewhere in the world of inventive forms of debt, the international fixed-income market offers investors an opportunity to diversify their portfolios, mitigate currency risk, and reap a higher rate of return than local debt securities offer. Downside: they also carry a greater risk of default, especially when linked to developing countries.

International fixed-income instruments can include global bonds, foreign bonds, and Eurobonds. A global bond refers to a type of bond issued in multiple countries at the same time, usually by a multinational corporation or sovereign entity with a strong credit rating and huge capital requirements. A global bond issued by a US entity in China will be denominated in Chinese yuan. A Chinese company selling bonds in the US will promise to pay back in US dollars.

A Eurobond, meanwhile, refers to any bond denominated in a currency other than that of the country where the bond was issued. A good example is a yen-denominated bond being sold in the European financial markets. Both individual and institutional investors can invest in international fixed-income through mutual funds or individual bonds.

Senior Rate Floating Notes, which usually are issued by firms with poor credit ratings, pay a variable interest rate generally tied to a money-market reference rate such as the Federal Funds Rate or LIBOR, plus a quoted margin. "Senior" refers to a promissory note that takes priority in payment should the issuer go bankrupt. In times of high interest rates, floating-rate notes have higher yields than fixed-rate notes, which are a better option in times of falling interest rates.

You can buy individual Senior Rate Floating Notes or invest through mutual funds and ETFs, as with so many other asset classes. They are especially worthy now as the Fed starts raising interest rates after a decade of dormancy. Currently the US economy is growing faster than the rate of 2 percent or so for the previous decades, and in an economy with stronger growth, interest rates tend to go up rather than down.

## Bond Risks Revisited

Bonds mistakenly are considered a *safe* investment because most times the investor gets his (or her) money back, especially in the case of bonds issued by various levels of government in the US. Yet bonds can plunge in price on sudden shifts in consumer sentiment, demand for stocks, and, most of all, changes in interest rates.

The truth is that bonds carry their own unique set of risks, and it is vital to understand each of them. Bonds are *safer* compared with some other investments, but less safe than others. Understanding bond risk is crucially important in these Fed-dominated days of the bond markets.

Though we have touched on bond risks earlier, it is a topic worth revisiting in detail here. Six major kinds of risk can affect your bond returns: maturity risk, interest rate risk, reinvestment risk, liquidity risk, ratings downgrade risk, and credit default risk. To break them down further:

*Maturity risk* may be the most important one. A bond is known as a fixed-income security because the investment pays a fixed rate of interest on the principal amount until a bond matures. Available maturities range from thirty days all the way up to thirty years. When you buy a bond, you are taking a risk that interest rates elsewhere might rise in the time you hold that bond. Buying a bond with a longer waiting period to maturity increases that risk.

So, if you buy a thirty-year bond that pays say, 6 percent, you may think of yourself as a genius, but if interest rates pop to 15 percent or higher (as they did in the late 1970s), then you will be kicking yourself. Alas, if you buy a short-term bond to reduce the chances of this happening, you aren't taking much risk, so you won't earn much yield. That's why it's a good idea to be diversified.

*Maturity risk premium* is the extra yield—the premium—you earn from buying a bond with a longer time to maturity. This notion of maturity risk premium exists any time you have an investment that pays a fixed interest rate and has a fixed maturity date. Is there some way to quantify maturity risk premium, so you can compare apples to apples? Yes. This risk premium can be quantified by comparing your chosen investment with investments with different maturities.

Say your bank pays 1 percent interest on a two-year certificate of deposit and 3 percent on a six-year certificate of deposit. You earn an extra two percentage points more per year, and three times the original interest rate, for tying up your money for three times as long. We see a real-world example looking at government bonds. The yield on the twenty-year Treasury recently was 2.33 percent, just when the yield on the thirty-year bond was 2.59 percent. Is it worth it to you to earn an extra 0.26 percent per year for giving the government a loan for those extra ten years? Unlikely.

When this spread narrows too much between ten-year bonds and thirty-year bonds, it prompts worries of a flattening yield curve, meaning the thirty-year return is unimpressively higher than the return on the ten-year bond on a chart plotting the curve of interest rates for tens versus thirties. An inverted yield curve, when shorter-term bonds are paying *higher* rates than thirty-year bonds, makes investors worry that recession is nigh.

Now, how can you assess maturity risk premium if you don't know which way interest rates may go? That's the trickiest part of the deal. What we do know is this: interest rates have spent recent years at forty-year lows. They are more likely to rise than fall at this point. Consequently, you should be careful about locking yourself in to long-term maturities in the present environment. That is why many managers suggest you build a bond ladder.

In a bond ladder, you buy bonds with differing maturity dates—short-term, medium-term, and long-term in regard to when they come due—so that they form a ladder of tiered payouts spread over different spans of time. Bonds that mature in two months, three months, four months, one year, two years, and so on offer a panoply of payout possibilities.

As maturity dates arrive, you roll over the bond and buy it again at the same maturity. If interest rates have risen, you will take advantage of that because the newest bonds you acquire will offer the higher rates.

*Interest Rate Risk* is another factor that bears watching warily. Most conservative investors focus on a bond's yield and get excited when it is high compared with other investments' returns. Let's say you bought a ten-year, $1,000 bond today at a coupon rate of 5 percent per year, and interest rates in the meantime rise to 7 percent. What you once thought was a great coupon isn't looking so great anymore.

Rising interest rates make new bonds more attractive because they earn a higher coupon rate. Thus, another phrase for interest rate risk is *opportunity risk*, meaning there's a risk that a better deal will appear, and you can't take advantage of it. Thus, the longer the term of your bond, the greater the chance that interest rates elsewhere will rise in the meantime, sending your bond price down and costing you a shot at a newer, higher-rate bond.

It gets worse. Let's say you need to sell your 5 percent bond prior to maturity. If interest rates are higher, you now must compete with bonds paying a higher interest rate. This will decrease demand for bonds at 5 percent, forcing you to sell at below par, or less than you paid for it. The price gets pushed down.

The longer the duration of your bond, the more volatility it will experience in price. Any suggestion that interest rates may rise could send the price of your long-term bond down significantly. That is yet another reason why long-term bonds earn higher interest rates—because there is more risk the bond price will decline over time.

Bond fund managers face the same risks as individual bondholders. When interest rates rise—especially when they go up sharply in a short period of time—the value of the fund's existing bonds drops, which can put a drag on overall fund performance.

Historically, we see interest rates rise when the economy is growing robustly and prices generally are on the rise, and we see rates decline in downturns. That's because in bad times, business demand for credit is slack and banks' willingness to lend is scant, so the government tries to induce businesses to invest by cutting interest rates to make borrowing cheaper. Also, rising inflation leads to rising interest rates, and declining inflation leads to lower interest rates.

*Reinvestment risk,* the third kind of bond risk, is the threat of interest rates going down, and investors having to reinvest their principal or their bond income at a lower interest rate than before.

Suppose you buy a bond paying 5 percent. Reinvestment risk will affect you if interest rates drop and you have to reinvest the regular interest payments at 4 percent. Reinvestment risk will also apply if the bond matures and you have to reinvest the principal at less than 5 percent. Reinvestment risk will not apply if you intend to spend the regular interest payments or the principal at maturity.

*Liquidity risk* is the risk that if you need to sell in a hurry, you could be unable to find a buyer. This risk rises when smaller companies sell corporate bond issues that are so thinly traded that finding a rare buyer for your bond may require lowering your price even more than you had planned.

*Rating downgrade risk* is the risk that while you hold a bond, one of the big ratings agencies will downgrade that company's credit rating, which could raise uncertainty about the company's ability to finance operations and generate cash to make its bond payments as required. The price of your bond could fall instantly, causing a loss if you end up selling.

*Credit default risk* is the ever-present possibility that the bond you bought might default, and the money you offered up front will never get paid back. For bonds overall this risk is rather low, yet the mere *fear* of interest rate swings can spook investors and cause them to flinch and sell, sending bond prices down as much as any real shift in rates on any given day.

\* \* \*

When you buy a $100,000 Treasury bond that promises to pay you 2 percent interest annually for ten years, you may feel confident that your rate of return is 2 percent. In fact, it is something less than that once you factor in adviser fees, taxes, and other rogue interlopers that take their cut before you get to your real bottom line.

Never mind that Capital One ad slogan, "What's in your wallet?" The better question is, "What's your *real* rate of return?" The next chapter will explain that.

# CHAPTER 10

# Real Rate of Return

For my first decade at Morgan Stanley & Co., I was a True Believer. Whatever the firm told me to do, I did it; whatever the firm said to believe, I believed in earnest; and when Morgan Stanley gave me a list of mutual funds and ETFs to sell, I sold them. Only after an uncomfortable visit to the doctor did I learn that serving my firm's desires had distracted me from a more important consideration: what did my clients actually *need*?

By the early '90s, I had shown an adeptness for selling financial advice. Empathy for the client was a strong suit of mine, I felt, as was my willingness to bluntly point out the failings of rival firms. My faith in Morgan Stanley's products didn't hurt, either.

On one sales sweep into Tulsa, Oklahoma, I set up shop in a hotel near the airport and started cold-calling new prospects in the area. In those days what you coveted most of all was a print directory of a big company's employees, all of them potential clients. On this trip, I was fortunate to have a directory of Phillips Petroleum, and I picked up the phone in my hotel room and began calling company executives one by one.

This was how I came across Dr. Gene Whitener. I rented a car and drove an hour and a half from Tulsa to Bartlesville, Oklahoma, to pitch him my services. He let me into his modest home and led me down the hallway, past the living room, and into the kitchen, where we sat at the kitchen table and I began my spiel. I laid out brochures of various mutual funds and began describing them, when Dr. Whitener interrupted me and asked:

"Son, what do I need?"

"I don't know," I answered without hesitation; I knew only what I could sell him. "That's right," he said, "because you never asked. If you don't have the wherewithal to ask what I need, how can you help me?" He then politely asked me to leave and ushered me out.

Only later did I learn that he was retiring on $4 million. He was a widower with no children, and he "needed" only $400 a month to cover his living expenses. Those facts changed the picture dramatically, yet most financial planners proceeded like I had, without answering that most basic question: what does the client need? Lesson learned. Ultimately, I landed Dr. Whitener as a client, parking some of his money in managed futures as a hedge against the main investments in his portfolio.

At the most respected firms on Wall Street, they would have you believe that the focus is on serving your individual needs, when often the firm's upside is just as important a consideration; they sell you their products because they make more money on them.

When a Wall Street Goliath conjures up a new investment fund, say, or a new senior note with guaranteed annual returns, it wants to peddle this to investors to reap up-front fees that will then recur every year. Senior management at headquarters passes out an allocation of the new product to the regional directors and chiefs, who push the wares to their thirty to forty branch managers. Each manager then puts the touch on his twenty or thirty financial advisers: how much of this can you handle for us? Zero is an unacceptable answer; try again.

An old broker friend of mine refers to this as "The Clipboard," the boss of the office going from rep to rep and keeping a tally of who was signing on to sell how much of the new product—without a microsecond of attention paid to asking, does this fit my client's needs? The biggest producers could win an all-expenses-paid trip to the Bahamas on a luxury cruise ship, or land a special bonus for selling their firms' newest investment scheme—an upside that usually was kept secret from their clients.

Other times, we brokers had to be willing to sell our clients new shares in a dull secondary offering of stock in a particular company, as a quid pro quo for the brokers' getting access later to the hottest new stocks just going public. All too often, serving ourselves, rather than our clients, was the real driver. I recall one day when, just as the market closed, we Morgan brokers received instructions to sell out a hundred thousand shares of a secondary stock offering for something called Plum Creek Timber. That night. And though we knew nothing about the company or why its shares might be suitable for our clients, we sure as hell did sell it to them.

Never mind whether the stock did well. Clients would think that we had a master plan for their portfolios and that Morgan Stanley had just alerted us to an urgent "buy" they must add to their holdings. In reality, our urgency and what we are shilling for often have more to do with the firm's agenda than with the clients' considerations. It always has been this way, and most investors are unaware of it. It is time to wake up and realize that practices like this go on all the time in the financial advice business.

These practices go undetected by clients because investors are so intently focused on one thing: how much money their portfolio can earn in returns. They monitor how much is coming in at the front end and neglect to pay attention to how much money is going out in the process, how much is being lost to drains such as taxes and fees and commissions that are the true goal of Wall Street. Exorbitant spending is one big drain, and if your increase in the cost of living is eclipsing your investment returns, you may want to fix your portfolio *and* move to a cheaper place to live; the combination of the two moves could save you from financial strain, or even ruin.

Another kind of drain is more insidious. It creeps up on you sight unseen and takes such a skinny sliver of your returns that you barely notice it, or don't care if you do. Yet this sliver can compound, adding up to a significant drag on your results over a few decades. I'm talking about the slow, silent scourge of inflation and the real price increases in your cost of living. Your personal inflation rate likely is bigger than the government CPI says it is, and that undercuts the returns in your account.

Taxes also are a big drain on the returns of a portfolio outside your retirement account. Other gremlins in the system also take their cut: management fees, investment fees, and administrative expenses. Fix a few flaws here and you can save thousands of dollars over a period of thirty years, or maybe hundreds of thousands of dollars if your account is at seven figures or more.

Only after determining what your portfolio is losing to these forces can you know how your account truly is faring, bottom-line.

In a previous chapter, all of the discussion of *standard deviation* and how it was derived from ten years of real results involved the *gross rate of return*. This is how much your investments earned before you had to pay certain costs of the investing, before deducting fees, expenses, and taxes. Once you have revved down your account's standard deviation as much as possible while ensuring adequate returns, you then can focus on whittling down fees and expenses, too.

Start with the simple assumption that if your investments began the year with a total value of $100,000 and ended at $115,000, you made a 15 percent return. The more complicated answer—and keep in mind that on Wall Street, complicated matters drive more fees for advice and strategies on how to handle them—is that your *gross* return was 15 percent, but that is just for starters.

The real question is what was your *real rate of return*, after you lost invisible slivers of your assets to inflation, taxes, and fees. Often we invest in a mutual fund or ETF while paying scant attention to whether there was a starting fee (a "load" in mutual fund parlance) to buy it, and with little idea of whether the annual fees we pay amount to 1 percent of our investment or just 0.1 percent per year. Yet the difference between those two numbers is enormous, and compounded over four decades (from your twenties to your sixties), the money you save or squander can add up to hundreds of thousands of dollars.

The little stuff counts, and always remember the best way to get rich is to hold on to what you already have, rather than making huge, risky bets on something that might pay off big-time. Cut your expenses and spending, save and invest more, and accept consistent, middling returns to reduce your risk and protect against big losses. It is like good barbecue and smoking techniques: low and slow and steady until it's ready (and now I shall cease and desist with the cooking metaphors as they make me hungry).

You want to be able to maintain your current standard of living for the rest of your life, right? You want to avoid being forced to settle for less, possibly a lot less, because your investments fell behind the increase in your cost of living each year. My goal is to make sure investors know exactly how much money they need to maintain their purchasing power, from today until they die.

This level of directness is rare on Wall Street, where things are intentionally obtuse, cloaked in camouflage so that advisers can speak in generalities without getting tied down to the details. I say let us cut to the chase: how much better is your life after taxes, after fees, after the increase in your cost of living? Has your financial adviser helped make your life better? The big Wall Street firms never tell you that. People need to know their real rate of return; it is time for them to get *real*.

The problem is that neither brokers nor money managers have any idea what "real rate of return" is or how to construct a portfolio to achieve a better one. So, let's break it down.

## Real Rate of Return

A *rate of return* is the amount of money you gain or lose on an investment in a set period of time, expressed as a percentage of the investment's cost. So, if you invest $1,000 in a stock, and you sell it for $1,100, you have a *rate of return* of 10 percent. This is where most investors stop asking questions and where most wealth managers *want* them to stop asking questions.

All rate of return tells you is how much you made on your investment at first glance. It stops short of telling you anything about how much *risk* you took to make that money or the expenses and other costs involved. Deduct those and you have your *real rate of return*. For now, remember this formula:

*Real Rate of Return = Gross Rate of Return − management fees, taxes, and cost-of-living increase.*

*Real Rate of Return* is the metric to watch in calculating whether your investments are spinning off enough gains and dividends each year to protect you from losing ground to the rising prices in your part of the world. It answers the question: what do I have left? After taxes and fees and the like, are you still ahead and building wealth, or are you falling behind?

That's where my CHIP Score comes in. It will help you figure out what real rate of return is adequate to protect your purchasing power. The process begins by investing for *Gross Return*, usually by investing in one or more of three areas: an income-producing security, a security geared more toward capital growth (the rising price of the investment), or an alternative vehicle.

*Income* investments come with some form of assurance you will get the money you invested returned to you at some point. Somebody or some company promises to pay you back, therefore the risk is lower, which means you must settle for a lower return. These investments involve some form of borrowing. They are loans of some kind. So the amount you originally invested is not going to *grow*. You will get that same amount back at some point, collecting some kind of return on your loan as *interest* or *dividends* or *distributions*.

For example, you might loan money to a friend and have a promissory note as the promise to repay. In exchange for this loan, your friend pays you interest. A bank might loan money to you to buy a house, which, of course, is called a mortgage. In exchange for this loan, you promise to repay the bank over thirty years and in the meantime pay it interest for taking on the risk of handing you the loan.

The city where you live might issue municipal bonds that investors from all over the world can buy, which transfers their money to your city, allowing it to be used for a specific purpose. The city promises to repay the bondholders in several years, along with interest each year as compensation for taking on the risk of loaning money to the city.

*Growth* investments come in many forms, but usually involve actual ownership of something, such as a small piece of a company, otherwise known as shares of stock. It could be real estate. It could be shares in a mutual fund. With growth, you have unlimited upside. You might invest in a restaurant business that specializes in cheesecake. Twenty years later, this restaurant becomes a chain called The Cheesecake Factory, because it kept growing and growing. Now the piece of that company you purchased is worth much more than it was originally.

Then again, you could lose your entire investment. Maybe you invested in an electronics chain called Circuit City, which fell to intense competition from Best Buy on one front (brick-and-mortar) and Amazon.com on another (online). It disappeared and its stock went to zero, and your investment ended up being worth nothing.

While a stock's price is supposed to offer enough growth to compensate holders for the higher risk they take on by buying it, once a company stumbles and bankruptcy looms, it plunges—often declining well before anyone knew the company was in trouble.

The third category of investments, alternatives, includes private equity, hedge fund strategies, and venture capital investments. It is best to mix and match investments from all three buckets (income, growth, alternative) and figure out the best proportions to serve your realistic target for returns, given your appetite for risk (or your aversion to it).

Why mix investments? Because you want to avoid tying yourself down to just one type of investment. If you are all in on stocks and the market crashes, but bonds hold up and alternatives do well in the same period, you will have put all your eggs in the worst basket. By diversifying, you put some money into each kind of investment to protect yourself, because each one has a different level of risk.

You can't totally decide this allocation until 1) you figure out the best mix, based on historical performance and an assessment of where things are headed; and 2) you factor in your expenses and taxes. A realistic expectation for real rate of return is about 10 percent annually when investing in public securities. That has been the average, roughly speaking, since 2000. That is a reasonable benchmark to set as your target.

So, now we know that we want to have three categories of investment so we can earn a gross rate of return. But how much of each kind of investment do we want in our portfolio? All investors invariably will say they want to earn the most money or get the highest gross return possible, with the least amount of risk. That's great, but how do you actually get there?

Everybody thinks brokers have some special sauce or magic ability to do it and that, if you are nice to them, they will let you in on the big secret. There is no big secret. This is where we get back to the importance of *Real Rate of Return*. My CHIP Score will help you figure out what it needs to be to hold on to your purchasing power. Using the CHIP Score, and based on history, you can figure out what percentage of a portfolio should be dedicated to growth vs. income vs. alternatives.

## Management Fees and Taxes

Now, we're going to look at the expenses that deduct from gross rate of return. Management fees and taxes are two of the three main expenses you subtract from gross rate of return to find the real rate of return. Management fees are the amount you pay your money manager or registered investment adviser to manage your portfolio.

In the early days, management fees were 2 percent of total assets managed. Today, they are down to 0.25 percent to 0.50 percent.

There's another type of management fee. Most portfolio managers will invest part of your money in a fund managed by a third party, and for this apparent honor you must pay a "sub-advised fund." The fees on these funds can vary widely. A hot-handed hedge fund manager may charge 2 percent of the total assets placed with him plus 20 percent of any profit the fund generates. Other funds are targeted to invest in only certain kinds of stocks, such as Small-Cap Value or Large-Cap Growth, and their fees hover around .010 percent to 1.5 percent.

Again, while the difference between those two numbers looks minuscule, in fact it is significant, especially when compounded over twenty or thirty or forty years. Obviously, you want low fees, but you also want the best-managed fund, as far as meeting your desire for a certain real rate of return, and one that reflects your risk profile.

Always ask your manager to specify what fees he charges and what fees any sub-advisers charge. No fee ever should be higher than 1 percent, except certain hedge funds and private equity funds, many of which had cut their fees in half after the meltdown of 2008 and have raised fees steadily back up toward their previous highs.

*Taxes* take an even bigger bite out of your investment gains than management fees. We all hate taxes, and one of the challenges of structuring any portfolio is making certain it is tax-efficient for each individual investor. If there's a lot of buying and selling in your portfolio, your broker is running up trading commission fees and may be generating a ton of capital gains, on which you will have to pay taxes.

If you are in a high tax bracket, even a good gross rate of return can be eaten away by taxes. At first glance, you might turn to tax-free bonds to sidestep the tax burden, yet a taxable bond of a lower investment grade can pay an interest rate much higher than the tax-free bond. If you lose 40 percent of your earnings to taxes, you would require a taxable bond paying 3.33 percent to match the tax-free returns of a 2 percent tax-free bond.

This is one reason that investing inside your retirement account is paramount, allowing your principal to grow—tax-free—for decades and then compounding on top of that ever-larger sum, making you richer and richer. The problem is that the government imposes limits on how much of your earnings you are allowed to tuck away, untouched for years to come.

* * *

You have educated yourself in alternative assets to balance out stock holdings—non-correlated assets, arbitrage strategies, and bonds; and you have learned to discount COLA, taxes, and fees to sift out your portfolio's real rate of return. Now, you are ready to take on a mission-critical skill in investing: asset allocation, up next in Chapter Eleven.

# CHAPTER 11

# Allocating Your Assets

Ever watch the cooking-competition show *Chopped* on the Food Network? Each of four rival chefs has twenty minutes to whip up an appetizer. The judges "chop" one chef, then eliminate a second one after the entrée round, and get down to the winner by dessert.

Each round features a new "mystery basket" of oddball ingredients all the chefs must use, such as Rocky Mountain oysters, squid ink, fiddlehead ferns, or Buddha's hand (a fruit). Yet the chefs turn out an amazing array of dishes with wildly divergent recipes, using components in different proportions and different ways. Coming up with the best combination is what wins the $10,000 prize at the end of each show.

The same idea applies to the lengthy list of types of asset classes in which you can invest. It astonishes me (and disturbs me) how most portfolios are overly invested in the usual suspects—stocks and bonds, either separately or tucked into mutual funds and ETFs—and lacking in so many other contrarian, non-correlated ingredients.

It is wise to start adding these against-the-grain assets to your life savings, though the question arises: which ones and in what proportions?

This is what we call *asset allocation*. It is the key to good investing, requiring an understanding of the correlations among various kinds of assets, an acknowledgement that the world of correlations has changed, and the admission that what used to work doesn't work anymore.

A lot of firms on Wall Street have fallen short in adjusting to this shift. (See Chapter Seven on non-correlated assets.) Should alternative investments compose 50 percent of your holdings or only 33 percent, or maybe just 10 percent? Coming up with the right recipe for your mix of assets is an elusive black art and a mystery to most Wall Street firms.

Your typical broker is likely to advise you based on the old saw about splitting stocks and bonds based on the result of 110 minus your age: if you are age fifty, then 110 minus fifty equals sixty, so 60 percent of your portfolio should be in stocks. The portion in stocks goes down as you age because you have fewer years remaining for your depressed portfolio to recover from steep losses.

That is a fine place to start, though this split underestimates the upside power of stocks over the long term, and it fails to recognize that we live much longer than we did even a few decades ago, so we have more time for a rebound. You must go much further in constructing a sound portfolio. Yet, everywhere I looked on Wall Street, I found all of us were operating without a real guide for doing this.

Most of us were failing to weigh returns against the risk we were injecting into client portfolios, failing to reduce volatility and the range of possible outcomes, failing to brace our clients for the effects of the unseen increase in their cost of living, and failing to ensure our clients were adding off-the-beaten-path, non-correlated assets to their accounts.

When I gave away most of my smaller accounts in the late '90s to focus on building my first "bill," I joined an elite group of wealth advisers. My hope was they would possess a higher level of knowledge and preparation than the rank-and-file brokers, but what I found instead was more of the same.

Certainly the vocabulary was more advanced for the advisers in this realm of the swells, as I learned when I started working on mergers and acquisitions at Morgan Stanley. Yet these higher beings in banking still possessed the same blind spots on COLA, risk, and volatility. None of them were following a set of well-tested guidelines for what kinds of investments should make up the typical asset allocation for which kinds of clients. Asset allocation was, like the rest of it, more of an afterthought.

I saw the wider problem after I quit Morgan Stanley and joined Bank of America (B of A) months later, in early 2003. Upon arrival at B of A, I embarked on an introductory tour around the empire to meet with various luminaries, all of whom were knowledgeable and impressive—and every bit as vague on asset allocation as the rest of us on the Street. At one point I flew to St. Louis to meet with one of the smartest people I ever have met in the investment banking world: Dr. Joseph Cherian, who, at this point, was at Banc of America Capital Management.

He had a bachelor's degree in electrical engineering from the Massachusetts Institute of Technology (MIT), and a master's and PhD in finance from Cornell University. A year or two after we met, he would take a job at Credit Suisse in New York to run $67 billion in alternative assets—how's that for a "bill"? He was one brilliant guy, and yet even Joe Cherian didn't have some secret, magical system for allocating assets and evaluating risk and volatility in a portfolio.

He acknowledged the industry's silence on this issue, and I told him there should be some sort of formula, a way to measure all portfolios to determine how well they were serving their clients in terms of allocation and diversification, risk and volatility, cost-of-living increase and more. There's nothing like that, he told me back then.

That was my *eureka!* moment, and it made me think that I needed to create something like that. You can rate your driver on Uber, rate a restaurant on Yelp, buy a washer-dryer with an energy rating, and scroll through Consumer Reports for ratings on thousands of products—yet nowhere is there a cogent, consumer-friendly rating system for how we invest trillions of dollars in life savings for millions of people. Thus began the years-long creation of the CHIP Score.

At the time, Joe Cherian and I were talking about the flaws of the Sharpe ratio, a financial metric for rating and comparing the returns of hedge funds that gets bandied about a lot by advisers talking to institutional investors.

The Sharpe ratio often is used to compare two different kinds of assets with different rates of return, say, an international stock fund versus a basket of utility stocks, to help the investor pick the one that offers a solid return with less volatility. The metric is applied to entire portfolios, too.

At first glance, the Sharpe ratio seems to do a good job of assessing returns compared with the risks involved in earning them. Economist William F. Sharpe devised the ratio in 1966 as a simple way to compute this relationship between risk and returns. In 1990 he won the Nobel Prize in Economic Sciences for his work in creating the capital asset pricing model, which calculates an asset's rate of return against its market risk, compared with the expected return of a theoretical risk-free asset.

To compute the Sharpe ratio, you start with an asset or fund's rate of return for the previous decade or more—say it is 10 percent. You subtract from this number the rate of return offered by a risk-free asset, usually three-month Treasury bills, which lately have paid annual interest of 1.89 percent. So 10 percent minus 1.89 percent equals 8.11 percent—this is how much more in returns you earned by taking on the extra risk you assumed above and beyond the almost risk-free rate on three-month T-bills.

Next, you take that extra-risk return of 8.11 percent and divide it by the *standard deviation* of your portfolio. Say your portfolio had a standard deviation of eight for that gross annual return of 10 percent; so that 95 percent of the time in the past decade, your results fell somewhere in the range of up 26 percent (10+8+8=26) and down 6 percent (10-8-8=[-6]), finishing with an average of 10 percent in any given year. Now divide that 8.11 percent risk-on-return by the standard deviation of eight and you get a Sharpe ratio of 1.01.

Fantastic! A Sharpe ratio of one or higher is considered excellent, and wealth advisers make a big deal out of it when selling a hedge fund to their clients. They will offer you two hedge funds and tell you the first one has a Sharp ratio of only 0.5, but the second one—take a look at this baby—it has a 1.2 Sharpe ratio! As if it has superhuman strength, it's the Incredible Hulk.

So, if Mrs. McGuilicutty has a portfolio posting an average annual return of 4 percent with a standard deviation of two that would produce a Sharpe ratio of 1.05, it is supposed to be just dandy. Yet her portfolio is a disaster because it is returning 4 percent and she lives in Dallas, where her costs really are rising closer to 7 percent a year.

She is falling behind at a frightful pace, every year, and the Sharpe ratio gives her portfolio an excellent rating, because *it fails to take COLA into account at all*. That is a prescription for a long, slow, imperceptible slide into financial suicide. Yet, here we are, telling the client to take comfort in knowing her portfolio has a great Sharpe ratio.

It is like saying "These go to eleven," as the vapid, gum-chewing lead guitarist Nigel Tufnel put it, spinning the knobs on an amplifier in the mockumentary *This is Spinal Tap*. It means nothing.

Sharpe also fails to assess another risk to your returns—volatility, and the emotional and unwise responses that it can create. Volatility hurts in two ways, once when it causes an asset's value suddenly to plunge, and a second time when that plunge or the news of it causes an investor to do something stupid in response.

The Sharpe ratio is better used for institutional portfolios, whose managers have less emotional responses to volatility because they take what is happening to their accounts less personally—it is other people's money at risk.

What about the individual investor, though? Somebody should devise an intelligent, sophisticated portfolio evaluation method for the little guy, a scoring system that will reveal whether your financial adviser is ensuring your asset allocation is optimal and your targeted returns will offset your higher cost of living. No one has done it. Yet.

At one point some years ago, I gave a speech to three hundred advisers at a Merrill Lynch gathering, and I asked those in the audience to raise their hands if they knew the definition of the Sharpe ratio. Maybe forty people raised their hands. Then I asked how many knew what a good Sharpe ratio is, and three people responded. Merrill's literature talks plenty about the Sharpe ratio, yet clearly the firm does little to train its brokers in the details of it.

Wall Street was failing to train its advisers in proper portfolio construction and asset allocation, so I turned my gaze to regulators. Maybe they were better positioned to gauge risk and ensure that Wall Street was following appropriate asset allocation guidelines and issue warnings when things got out of hand. So, a few months before the Great Meltdown of 2008, I began researching what the Securities and Exchange Commission and the industry's self-regulatory body, FINRA (Financial Industry Regulatory Authority), were doing to rein in risk, erect boundaries for safe asset allocation, and stop Wall Street giants from leading their lemming clients off a cliff.

Alas, the SEC and FINRA were doing little to nothing on this front. My research showed the SEC was focused on making sure Wall Street followed the rules, while FINRA was more devoted to ensuring Wall Street didn't get sued or investigated by the SEC. Both agencies were silent on proper asset allocation and the right level of risk and how to quantify it.

At one point, I went so far as to contact FINRA directly. Someone patiently listened to my points about how they were clueless on these concerns. I offered to visit her and lay out how FINRA should evaluate investor risk and set parameters for allocating assets in a portfolio. She told me to go pound sand, basically. FINRA had no interest whatsoever in my views.

This left me stunned and walking around in a daze for the next week. If the regulators didn't have a system for evaluating portfolio risk and asset allocation, why would the Wall Street wealth advisers under their watchful eye be able to understand it, much less their clients?

This was a disaster waiting to happen, and it felt as though everyone on Wall Street was in on it. So many people in the business were faking it and getting away with it, perpetuating a lie that they had your back when they didn't, and everyone believed them. And we were doing nothing to fix it. I felt like a fraud.

Around 2012 I had some key elements of my new CHIP Score system in place and I wanted to test them, so I went calling on the biggest names on Wall Street with a simple request: please show me your model portfolios. I wanted to see how they approached asset allocation, by what formula they divvied up client funds into various types of vehicles.

Fidelity Investments, J. P. Morgan Chase, Citigroup, Goldman Sachs, Merrill Lynch, UBS—the premiere shops on Wall Street were proud to show me their model portfolios. I ran them through some of my new metrics—standard deviation, level of risk and volatility, how much money a portfolio could lose if enough things went wrong.

The results stunned me. Virtually all of these supposedly safe, low-risk model portfolios were, in fact, geared to take on far higher risk—and the possibility of far higher losses—in any given year than any investor should find acceptable. The asset allocation of every one of the portfolios I inspected was aggressive in risk-taking based on historical rate of return versus standard deviation. Even the models labeled conservative were aggressive.

Yet these model portfolios and asset allocations were constructed by the best minds on Wall Street. Unbelievable.

The model portfolios were horrible! Some were described as "low-risk," yet nowhere was it disclosed as to what this meant. Some portfolios had a 26 percent chance of losing money in any given twelve-month period, based on historical data. Nobody would call that "low-risk."

Take a look at the numbers for these four model portfolios from four different financial titans, each portfolio based on a starting investment of $3 million in total. In most cases they carry more risk and downside than advertised.

## Morgan Stanley Conservative

| METRICS | PORTFOLIO |
|---|---|
| Starting Value | $3,000,000 |
| Rate of Return | 6.61% |
| Standard Deviation | 6.39% |

| METRICS | RESULTS |
|---|---|
| Variance Drag Phantom Tax | 0.97 |
| Sharpe Ratio | 0.88 |
| Probability of Loss in Next Twelve Months | 15% |
| Amount of Money at Risk in Next Twelve Months | $247,661 |
| Upper Return | 19.36% |
| Lower Return | -6.17% |

When I reviewed the metrics for the conservative portfolio of Morgan Stanley, the numbers were pretty good, for starters. The Morgan Stanley Conservative portfolio had a rate of return of 6.61 percent and its standard deviation was lower than its average return, at 6.39. (Recall that when it comes to STDs, the lower, the better. If you can get the STD less than your average rate of return, as is true in this case, it is great.)

The chart above lists a new metric we haven't yet explained: the Variance Drag Phantom Tax. I invented it and we will go into the details of this metric in the next chapter. For present purposes, just know that the Drag Phantom Tax is the ratio of your account's standard deviation to its rate of return (STD divided by RoR), and it should be at less than 1.0. In this Morgan fund's case, the VDPT is 0.97—that's good. The probability of producing a loss in any given twelve-month period is restrained at 15 percent, my recommended limit, and the worst you can do likely will be down 6 percent or so in a year's time—a relatively low downside.

## Bank of America/Merrill Lynch Moderate

| METRICS | PORTFOLIO |
|---|---|
| Starting Value | $3,000,000 |
| Rate of Return | 3.86% |
| Standard Deviation | 12.60% |

| METRICS | RESULTS |
|---|---|
| Variance Drag Phantom Tax | 3.27 |
| Sharpe Ratio | 0.23 |
| Probability of Loss in Next Twelve Months | 38% |
| Amount of Money at Risk in Next Twelve Months | $765,653 |
| Upper Return | 29.12% |
| Lower Return | -21.40% |

Merrill Lynch's "moderate" model portfolio, conversely, is all too risky. Its standard deviation should be at 80 percent or less of its average annual return, yet this portfolio has an STD of 12.6—three to four times as high as its annual return. This model's Drag Phantom Tax is a hugely damaging 3.27, and the portfolio carries almost a 40 percent chance of running a loss in any twelve-month period, way too high.

Likewise, the Growth and Income portfolio for Goldman Sachs has a standard deviation at more than double its rate of return (it should be 4.8 rather than 15.2), which means it has way too much volatility. It also boasts a rather high phantom tax at 2.42 and a one-in-three chance of losing money in any given year. Plus, the maximum downside is steep: a loss of almost $900,000, potentially.

## Goldman Sachs Growth/Income

| METRICS | PORTFOLIO |
|---|---|
| Starting Value | $3,000,000 |
| Rate of Return | 6.27% |
| Standard Deviation | 15.20% |

| METRICS | RESULTS |
|---|---|
| Variance Drag Phantom Tax | 2.42 |
| Sharpe Ratio | 0.35 |
| Probability of Loss in Next Twelve Months | 34% |
| Amount of Money at Risk in Next Twelve Months | $872,715 |
| Upper Return | 36.67% |
| Lower Return | -24.13% |

## JP Morgan Chase Growth and Income

| METRICS | PORTFOLIO |
|---|---|
| Starting Value | $3,000,000 |
| Rate of Return | 4.50% |
| Standard Deviation | 16.67% |

| METRICS | RESULTS |
|---|---|
| Variance Drag Phantom Tax | 3.70 |
| Sharpe Ratio | 0.21 |
| Probability of Loss in Next Twelve Months | 39.36% |
| Amount of Money at Risk in Next Twelve Months | $1,028,407 |
| Upper Return | 37.84% |
| Lower Return | -28.84% |

J. P. Morgan Chase's portfolio for Growth and Income is even worse. Its rate of return, at 4.5 percent, is 28 percent lower than the 6.27 percent return of the Goldman Sachs portfolio, yet the standard deviation is even higher at almost seventeen, and so is the phantom tax, at a daunting 3.7 when 0.8 or lower is an ideal score. Worse yet, the J. P. Morgan model portfolio boasts almost a 40 percent chance of posting a loss in any twelve-month period—and the account could lose more than a million dollars in a single year. Ouch!

Always keep in mind: anytime we talk about a 40 percent probability of "a loss in any given twelve-month period," it always means a loss could happen two or even three years in a row. Loss-loss-loss. Enough to wipe out your life savings.

Moreover, whenever I talked to the people involved with building and maintaining these model portfolios, nobody could even quantify risk. I reviewed the components of three different Fidelity portfolios, one labeled conservative, the second one deemed moderate, and the third said to be aggressive—and every one of them was higher-risk than their labels would imply.

Et tu, Fidelity? The gigantic firm has almost $7 trillion in assets under management for twenty-seven million Americans, and it has a great reputation for safe, conservative investing. And even Fidelity approached clients as if they were fat-cat "whales" at the baccarat tables in Macau.

This surprising realization reinforced my disillusionment with Wall Street, and it showed me yet again that my industry was basically a big joke. This made me redouble my efforts to build a better method for evaluating portfolios and their asset allocation and, more importantly, a way to assess the performance of the advisers who design them. The new CHIP scoring system I devised is the answer.

And we are almost to the point where I reveal it, but first, a few broad strokes on the right asset allocation for your portfolio. In the old days journalists used the inverted pyramid to guide the unfolding of their stories, with the biggest and most important elements at the top followed by a succession of ever less important facts. And so it is with my Inverted Pyramid of Investing, which sets out the big-picture boundaries of asset allocation:

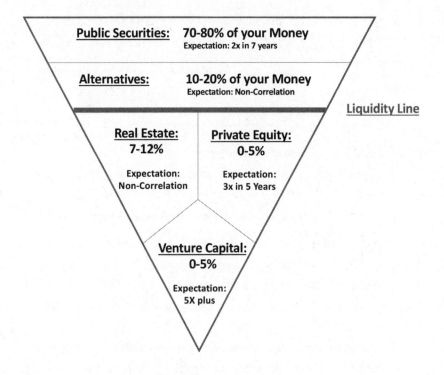

To elaborate on the obvious: typically 70 percent to 80 percent of your total assets should be in public securities (stocks, ETFs, mutual funds, and bonds, if you must, though bonds almost always lose purchasing power amidst a rising Consumer Pricing Index). Shoot for a return of 10 percent per year so as to double your money in 7.2 years, thanks to the miracle math of compounding.

Next up: Alternative assets for non-correlation purposes, to even out the wild sings of the stocks in your portfolio. Park 10 percent to 20 percent of your money here, with the expectation being one of non-correlation rather than a net upside return each year.

The "liquidity line" separates the readily accessible assets at the top of the inverted pyramid (public securities and alternatives) from other investments at the bottom, which lock up your money for years at a time and therefore are illiquid and unavailable.

In terms of what should comprise the alternative assets that occupy up to 20 percent of your portfolio, my recommendations break down as follows:

- *Real estate:* 7 percent to 12 percent of your portfolio for non-correlation to stocks
- *Private equity:* Zero to 5 percent of assets, with the goal of tripling your returns in five years
- *Venture capital:* Zero to 5 percent, at the very narrow, sharp tip of the upside-down investment pyramid, with the high expectation of losses and the aim of fivefold returns in five to ten years

There, I said it. Most financial advisers won't talk to you in these terms when discussing asset allocation, because if they start citing specific apportionments and percentages, you would be able to hold them accountable for what goes wrong in your account. Most advisers want to avoid that kind of scrutiny.

Millions of people have retirement accounts that are falling farther behind their COLA every day, forcing them to give up steak and settle for hamburger, and maybe dog food next, as John Williams put it (see Chapter 6). They face horrendous losses in the next market crash, unless they can learn ways to use asset allocation to their advantage, to reduce downside risks and narrow the range of outcomes in their accounts.

And it bears reiterating that another next market crash will come, eventually.

Chances are your Wall Street adviser has failed you on this front, and my goal is to empower you to fix this flaw yourself. You need a clear-cut way to assess your asset allocation, gauge how much risk you are taking on, and figure out whether your advisers are leading you to ruin. My CHIP Score is the answer, and in the next and final chapter of this book, you will learn many of its secrets.

# CHAPTER 12

# Deploying the CHIP Score

C ongratulations, you have earned it.

By making it this far into this book, you are ready to learn the secrets of my new CHIP Score system. It is a simple and clear way to assess and quantify the risk and volatility in your portfolio, and to determine whether you can reap the returns you need to keep pace with the rising prices in your life.

The CHIP Score can help you quantify your portfolio's range of outcomes, and it can estimate the chances your portfolio will produce a net loss in any given year. It even can tell you how much money you have at risk if everything goes wrong—and it can convert that vulnerability into actual dollars that could disappear.

Most important of all, the CHIP Score lets you evaluate the performance of your financial adviser and whether he or she is making you richer while preserving your assets, or unwittingly placing overly risky bets that could cost you dearly.

No other portfolio ranking or rating system can do these things. My new system marks the first time that investors can come up with a customized rating for how well their portfolios are serving their *individual* needs; it is the first method to let them take into account how much their individual cost of living is rising as a drag on their returns; and it is the first scoring system to let investors rate the performance of their advisers.

Brokers are going to hate that.

That is powerful stuff, and you cannot find this clarity anywhere else in the investing business. Nobody else on Wall Street, nor anywhere in Washington, has developed anything that comes close to it. I know this because I scoured the financial world for a scoring system like this one, consulting with some of the smartest minds at more than a dozen of the most powerful Goliaths on Wall Street. I interviewed brilliant professors and economists and contacted regulators at the SEC and FINRA.

Every time I came up empty.

This lapse is a sad and even scandalous situation, and it is by design. Financial advisers want to avoid offering you a hard-and-fast measure that points up their own failings. For years it has made me cringe that so many of my peers in wealth management have been giving out unwise, reckless advice, and selling model portfolios that hold far more risk of losses than they and their clients realize. All these financial advisers were constantly talking to their clients about things that were irrelevant, their clients having no idea how poorly trained the advisers really were.

So, I felt forced to create the CHIP Score because the industry clearly was refusing to do it. The CHIP Score can help investors vet their advisers—and expose their incompetence and call them out on it.

In this chapter, my aim is to equip you with the knowledge and understanding to deploy this new scoring system. Some of this will get a bit complicated, but we are talking about how you can best protect your wealth and support yourself for the rest of your life, maybe even leave something behind to help take care of those you love after you are gone. Learn it here, and it can pay off for you for years to come.

\* \* \*

Decades ago, people believed in their doctors blindly and rarely second-guessed their diagnoses and recommended remedies. Nowadays we have learned that the patient must get much more deeply involved in treatment decisions, doing his own research and making the final call.

Today most people approach their financial advisers with the same blind faith and unquestioning acceptance that they had afforded to their physicians so long ago—yet their financial advisers have far less training. This is a bad idea, given the mediocre quality of training, experience, creativity, and self-awareness in the overabundant ranks of brokers, advisers, wealth managers, insurance agents, business managers, investment advisers, and whatever other shingle any Tom, Dick, or Harry wants to hang up under the guise of managing other people's money.

I want clients to revolt against incompetence and neglect in my industry. If their advisers don't know what they are doing and won't take time to learn the business, I don't want them in my industry. The CHIP Score will empower you to evaluate how well or how badly your portfolio is performing based on your personal set of investment goals—and, as important, how well your *adviser* is performing for you. That startling insight might make many investors want to find a new wealth manager.

That, admittedly, is an extra reason why I offer the CHIP Score: it is good for my business. The other guys are clueless, and I can save you from them.

By now, you should have a better understanding of the important elements of investing that Wall Street fails to comprehend. My hope is that you know more about how to spot risk, reduce it, and narrow the array of possible investment outcomes (see Chapter Three). You even know about standard deviation, and that a narrower range is less risky than a wider one, and how your portfolio should have a standard deviation that is only 80 percent of your rate of return or less (see Chapter 4).

You also are newly aware that your personal COLA rate is two or three times the rate claimed by the Consumer Price Index (see Chapter Five). Also, you know why: because Washington tinkered with CPI to tamp down the COLA increases paid to more than sixty million people on Social Security (see Chapter Six). By now, you recognize the importance of adding non-correlated assets that can offset declines elsewhere in your portfolio (see Chapter Seven).

Given your new awareness of these things, everything you see in investing will look different when viewed through this new lens. The CHIP Score will help you get further down your path to financial security and successful investing. It is the product of thirty years of investing experience and listening to what clients want, their priorities and fears, through booming bull markets and jarring downturns and frightening, catastrophic crashes. This spans five boom-and-bust business cycles in all.

The CHIP Score can reveal a better way to invest, better at building the pillars that support a strong portfolio: smart risk assessment and reduction, keen awareness of real inflation and how to offset the damage it does, and sound construction and design. The wealth advisers in my business know almost nothing on these fronts, and they are unaware of their blind spot.

In pondering this scoring system, and devising and developing it and, finally, fine-tuning it and deploying it, I have created what may be the only approach that is personally tailored to take into account the individual client's COLA needs and the price increases of his lifestyle, as well as his income and tax burden, to figure out the necessary rate of return and how much risk he must take on to attain it.

Now, here is your opportunity to reap the benefits.

The CHIP Score will empower you to take a do-it-yourself approach to portfolio construction, so you can fix your retirement account and build it in a way that can make it all but impervious to the next market rout. Yes, your assets might go down in value when the next crisis descends, but you will take comfort in enduring less of a decline than the broad markets overall, because you will have diversified your assets, added contrarian investments, and insulated your account to reduce the downside possibilities.

The way I have designed the CHIP Score, the two most important factors it reflects are your personal inflation rate and volatility. Meaning the real increase in the cost of living your life at the standard you now maintain, and volatility meaning how wide is the range of possible things that can go right and things that could go wrong, and how much money could you lose if things got really hairy. Overall, 60 percent of the CHIP Score is based on the volatility in a portfolio, and 40 percent of the score is derived from the purchasing power that has been preserved in the account.

Best bet overall: Aim for a return of 10 percent a year with a standard deviation of eight. This would be enough in gains to cover your real COLA of, say, 7 percent a year and still come out ahead, with relatively low downside risk. If you can attain average annual returns of 10 percent, you can double your assets in roughly seven years.

You should limit the chances that your portfolio could lose money in any given year to 15 percent, which you can do by reducing the standard deviation of your account overall by subbing out riskier investments and adding lower-STD assets. Moreover, you should restrict your maximum downside loss to just 6 percent of total assets in a year (by having an account with a standard deviation of eight as it returns an average of 10 percent per year).

Lastly, once you retire, keep your annual spending at 4 percent or less of the total value of your retirement account. In investing, restraining your spending on the front end can boost the impact of your gains on the back end, no fancy risks required. Just as when a business cuts operating expenses, the savings flow instantly to the bottom line as dollar-for-dollar profits. Or when you are working out to lose weight, six-pack abs are made more in the kitchen (by reducing intake) than in the gym.

Recall that a portfolio with a 10 percent average annual return and an STD of eight means that, 95 percent of the time in the past ten years (and for two standard deviations), your portfolio returned an average of 10 percent a year and as much as 26 percent, or as low as down 6 percent, in any year. Given the broad stock market's long-term returns of 7.5 percent with a standard deviation of sixteen—too high an STD for your portfolio, overall—you will want to offset your seesawing stocks with non-stock investment vehicles that are less volatile and which boast a lower standard deviation.

Beneath the surface of the CHIP Score is a wealth of number-crunching algorithms assessing the risk and contents of each portfolio. All of this complexity is aimed at simplicity: the resulting score will fall in a range of zero to one hundred. If your portfolio has a score of seventy-five or higher, it is in great shape. A CHIP Score of fifty should have you concerned about some elements of risk and the potential for loss; and if your portfolio rates at a thirty or lower, you are in deep trouble, and it is time for an intervention. It means your portfolio has too much risk and volatility, too little diversification of assets, and returns that are falling short of your personal inflation rate.

You can use the CHIP Score to help your portfolio attain a better number. The process starts with your scoring your portfolio and where it stands currently. Thereafter, you can design your portfolio to hold a diversified mix of assets, non-correlating and otherwise, with varying levels of return and standard deviations and cascading maturity dates, and then figure out your new CHIP Score and how much it has improved. You can calculate all of this rather simply, and it starts by your filling in the answers to five main questions and eight major metrics, ranging from your assumed personal inflation rate to your tax rate, real rate of return, and standard deviation.

Go to my website at www.TheChipScore.com and you can even calculate your CHIP Score on the fly, and rejigger the various inputs to see how a few changes here or there can help you improve your account's score.

This clarity and simplicity are in stark contrast to the usual approach taken by wealth managers at the biggest Wall Street firms. If you have an investment adviser, wealth manager, or financial planner, you may have seen these spiffy reports that the big firms put together. They have fancy, colorful graphics and charts. They talk about the overall direction of the economy, and how each sector has performed and is expected to perform, and the real point is to show how smart they are supposed to be.

If you have been with your adviser for many years, you will get an update on where your assets are but not what your portfolio looks like in terms of risk, or whether your real rate of return can keep up with your personal COLA. That report, which you are paying for, is of absolutely no benefit to you, other than making it seem as though your adviser has a comprehensive investment plan for you.

The advisers ask questions about how much insurance you have, how many kids you have, what year you want to retire; they may talk about insulating you from taxes, and how to handle inheritances for your kids. From those answers, they will come up with some targeted rate of return necessary to "achieve your goals," and dictate a formula for your asset allocation, which, happily for their employers, will include mutual funds, ETFs, and bonds that their firms sell.

Once you approve this seemingly solid plan, the adviser gets to work, constructing a portfolio he has no idea how to construct, laying off his risk (but not yours) to outside managers and collecting fees in the meantime.

Along the way, your adviser never offers you a way to grade his or her performance, in part because the big Wall Street firms they represent have avoided coming up with a clear and simple way to measure their performance for their clients. They want to avoid such scrutiny.

There is a better way to do all of this, and it starts by knowing where your portfolio stands in terms of risk, returns, non-correlation, and other factors. By deploying the CHIP Score to vet the risk levels in your portfolio, you will know whether your assets are safe and whether they need more protection. Knowing this for certain, you can avoid reacting fearfully when markets suddenly plummet and panic overtakes opportunity. So your benefits are doubled: your assets are insulated from the worst downside, and this insulation lets you avoid responding emotionally and taking actions you might regret later.

Patience is a virtue, as the old saying goes (that one dates to the fourteenth century and English poet William Langland, Wikipedia says), and this especially is true in investing. Before you can learn how to figure out your CHIP Score and apply it to fixing your portfolio, you must learn a few things about the inputs that constitute this magical metric.

* * *

Tallying up your portfolio's CHIP Score begins with five key questions:

1. What is the total value of your portfolio?
2. What is the management fee as a percentage of the total portfolio?
3. What is the investment fee as a percentage of the total portfolio?
4. What is your income-tax bracket?
5. What is your estimated annual cost of living increase?

By deducting from the first number the next four numbers, you get your *Real Rate of Return* (see Chapter Ten), the first of eight key metrics that you must record as part of the process of building your CHIP Score. The others include:

- *Standard Deviation.* The span of risk vs. returns, the lower the number, the better. It should be at 80 percent or less of your average annual rate of return.

- *Variance Drag Phantom Tax.* This is the ratio of your standard deviation in proportion to your rate of return. You arrive at this number by dividing your portfolio's overall standard deviation by its average annual return. Ideally the VDPT should be less than your rate of return, and any drag phantom tax that is 150 percent of your return rate or higher (i.e., anything over a 1.5) is way too much risk.

- *Sharpe Ratio.* See Chapter Eleven. This measures risk-adjusted rate of return by subtracting the rate on a safe Treasury from your total rate of return to calculate how much extra profit you reaped on the extra risk; you then divide this adjusted return number by your account's standard deviation to get the Sharpe ratio. It should be one or higher for your entire portfolio; anything 0.5 or lower is unacceptable.

- *Loss Probability.* This should be 15 percent or less, meaning a 15 percent chance that your portfolio will experience any loss in the next twelve months. The CHIP Score calculator figures this out for you by running your list of assets through a *Monte Carlo simulation,* which crunches thousands upon thousands of investment return scenarios to come up with the odds of incurring a loss.

- *Money at Risk.* How much money you could lose in a year, in dollar terms, based on historical data for the previous ten-year period.

- *Upper and Lower Return.* The highest returns your portfolio could produce in a year compared with the worst returns possible for any given year, based on the previous ten-year period. You want this range of returns to be narrower rather than wider.

- *Correlation to S&P 500.* How closely a particular asset or sector in your portfolio mimics the movements of the broad large-cap stock index, on a scale of least similar (-1.0) to dead-on lockstep similarity (+1.0).

If you have attended a lot of weddings, you may have come across someone reading the biblical passage from Corinthians 13:13, which concludes, "So now faith, hope, and love abide, these three; but the greatest of these is love." The CHIP Score is less poetic; just know that of the eight measures listed above, the greatest of these is the *Variance Drag Phantom Tax.*

It sounds like a fee levied on a superhero in NYC's Village Halloween Parade, and I say this as the guy who made up the phrase. Yet as a pivotal component of the CHIP Score, it is well named: *Variance* for the wide variation in results, otherwise known as volatility; *Drag* for the restraint on your returns which volatility can cause; *Phantom Tax* for the invisible, pernicious, de facto tax on your returns posed by risk and volatility and the propensity to react to it, often wrongly.

Plus, Variance Drag Phantom Tax sounds kind of cool.

In essence, the VDPT quantifies how much risk and volatility you are assuming to get the best possible returns while losing the least on the downside. It should be restricted to be a lower number than the rate of return in your account. By now I have told you that your standard deviation should be no higher than 80 percent of your account's average annual returns, so that a 10 percent return should equate to a standard deviation no higher than eight. Similarly, the Variance Drag Phantom Tax should be at 0.8 times the account's rate of return or lower.

Those eight factors in hand, let us turn to the asset allocation in your portfolio and the makeup, mix, and extent of diversification. As you will see on TheChipScore.com, you are asked to fill in what percentage of your portfolio's value is invested in which of ten different kinds of asset classes. These include:

- Money market funds (tax-free cash and taxable cash);
- Fixed income (seven kinds of bonds, including government and high-yield);
- Hard assets (commodities, gold index, timber);
- US stock funds (twenty-three entries from emerging markets to large cap);
- International equities (four kinds);
- Utilities (ten major companies);
- Senior notes (nine choices);
- Business development companies (five fund picks);
- Alternative investment strategies (ten options including managed futures);
- Chapwood Managed Accounts (twenty-six different fund choices).

You are asked to enter a percentage of total assets for any of the assets on our list, and while this painstaking process could take you an hour or more, you will have to do this only once for the rest of your investing career. Thereafter, it will take you only a few minutes to make a few changes here and there, when needed. So...just do it, right?

\* \* \*

Now, let us review a few sample portfolios, find their CHIP Scores and compare and contrast them through this new lens. Sometimes seemingly similar portfolios with a similar rate of return can have startlingly different levels of risk and standard deviations.

### First Sample Portfolio

*Five Questions*

1. What is the total value of your portfolio, and its average annual return? $3 million, 10% per year

2. What is the management fee as a percentage of the total portfolio? 1%
3. What is the investment fee as percentage of the total portfolio? 1%
4. What is your income tax bracket? 32%
5. What is the estimated annual increase in your cost of living increase? 6%

Start with a 10 percent gross return. Less two percentage points in fees and six points in personal inflation and, already, this portfolio's *Real Rate of Return* is down to 2 percent. It is rather sobering, right? We aren't earning nearly as much on our investments as we believe. To calculate the first sample portfolio's CHIP Score, starting with the gross rate of return on a total fund of $3 million (I like to be optimistic), we add in the other metrics:

| METRICS | PORTFOLIO |
|---|---|
| Starting Value | $3,000,000 |
| Rate of Return | 9.19% |
| Standard Deviation | 9.30% |

| METRICS | RESULTS |
|---|---|
| Variance Drag Phantom Tax | 1.01 |
| Sharpe Ratio | 0.48 |
| Probability of Any Loss in Next 12 Months | 16.15% |
| Amount of Money at Risk in Next 12 Months | $373,351 |
| Maximum Upside in a Year | 27.79% |
| Maximum Downside in a Year | (-9.41%) |
| Cost of Living Increase | 6.00% |
| Tax Bracket | 32.00% |
| Real Rate of Return | 0.25% |
| Risk Free Rate | 1.00% |
| Management Fee Rate | 1.00% |
| Investment Fee Rate | 1.00% |
| CHIP SCORE | 55 |

Plug these numbers into the online calculator at www.TheChip-Score.com and you get your portfolio's CHIP Score: 55. That is a pretty good score. The maximum downside loss of 9.41 percent in a year is survivable; the drag phantom tax of 1.01 is containable (0.8 would be ideal). This portfolio's 16 percent chance of any loss in the next twelve months is acceptable.

Now let us look at a second example:

| METRICS | PORTFOLIO |
|---|---|
| Starting Value | $3,000,000 |
| Rate of Return | 7.58% |
| Standard Deviation | 10.90% |

| METRICS | RESULTS |
|---|---|
| Variance Drag Phantom Tax | 1.44 |
| Sharpe Ratio | 0.60 |
| Probability of Any Loss in Next 12 Months | 24.35% |
| Amount of Money at Risk in Next 12 Months | $533,316 |
| Maximum Upside in a Year | 29.38% |
| Maximum Downside in a Year | (-14.22%) |
| Cost of Living Increase | 6.00% |
| Tax Bracket | 32.00% |
| Real Rate of Return | 0.25% |
| Risk Free Rate | 1.00% |
| Management Fee Rate | 1.00% |
| Investment Fee Rate | 1.00% |
| CHIP SCORE | 22 |

This is a flawed portfolio. The probability of a loss in any given year is a startling 24.35 percent, which is almost one-in-four, and the maximum downside loss in any given year is almost twice the annual rate of return. The phantom drag is soaring at 1.44, 80 percent higher than it should be. Plus, the STD is significantly higher (at 140 percent of the rate of return).

Armed with my CHIP Score system, investors will have a straight-forward method for assessing their portfolios' performance on an array of fronts. This can help them have a pointed discussion with their investment advisers regarding whether their investments are holding their own against inflation and the rising costs in their own lives.

It is an outrage that the biggest names on Wall Street do such a bad job training their advisers to manage the wealth of their clients in safer, smarter ways. If these people are unable to do the job well and unwilling to get better at it, their clients should know enough to fire them. The CHIP Score will inform them.

As advisers we are obligated to make our clients' lives more secure financially, and this can free them from worry and let them live happier lives, generally. I take pride in my role in helping people secure a sustainable future for themselves and their families.

Every time I help another client shore up his portfolio and reduce unseen levels of risk, I feel good about it, and I think of my mom, Lois Tublin Butowsky, and how determined she was in the last year of her life, taking a job to keep pace with the rising costs eating away at her savings.

It was a long time ago, and she passed away before I could help her. In her memory, I am fortunate to be able to help others, and I am hope-ful my CHIP Score can help you, too. Risk and Reward is a far better way to go than risk, reward, and ruin. The CHIP Score can empower you to rate your adviser's performance and take control of your investing. It all is up to you—you must protect yourself.

# About the Author

Ed Butowsky is the founder and managing partner of Chapwood Investments in Plano, Texas, advising professional athletes, CEOs, entrepreneurs, and other investors in how to build and preserve their wealth. He spent eighteen years at Morgan Stanley & Co. before founding his own firm. He is a frequent markets guest on Fox News Channel, Fox Business Network, CNBC, and Bloomberg TV, and is known for his blunt and contrarian views.

Dennis Kneale is a writer and media strategist in New York. He started his career at *The Wall Street Journal*, served as managing editor of *Forbes* magazine, and was an anchor at CNBC and Fox Business Network. In the Great Meltdown of 2008, he urged viewers to resume buying stocks just one month after the market hit bottom, and in June 2009 he correctly predicted the end of the Great Recession and the recovery that followed.